THE ART OF PERFECT LIVING

THE ART OF PERFECT LIVING

The 7 Personal Powers for Perfection

Roby Jose Ciju

PARTRIDGE
A Penguin Random House Company

ISBN: Softcover   978-1-4828-2075-1
           Ebook   978-1-4828-2074-4

To order additional copies of this book, contact
Partridge India
000 800 10062 62
www.partridgepublishing.com/india
orders.india@partridgepublishing.com

CONTENTS

DEDICATED

To Dad, Mom, Ciju, Bobs, Sophy and Kuttu

To the entire Naduvileparampil Family of Cheruvandoor Parish, Kerala

To you, my readers, who, just like me, seek the path of perfection

INTRODUCTION

"Be ye therefore perfect, even as your Father which is in heaven is perfect."
(Matthew 5:48).

This passage from the Holy Bible tells us only one thing, *to be perfect* because our Father, in whose image we are created, is perfect. *What is Perfection?*

Perfection. A pursuit of a lifetime! We all want to lead a *'perfect'* life. We work hard all through our life to settle down comfortably with a perfect career, a perfect vehicle, a perfect house, a perfect spouse and of course, a perfect family, most probably in the same order. Then a point comes in our life where we have everything but we do not feel perfect. We search for a meaning in our life. In fact, we do not even know what we are searching for. *Is it perfection?*

The truth is no one in the world has so far come up with a standard for perfection. We do not know what this perfection is. Only thing that we do know is, we want to be perfect. *Just perfect.* And we all have our own perception about perfection. We all have our own standards of perfection.

However, almost all the Holy Scriptures, that are available across all the religions, have clearly defined a state of 'perfection' in a human life. The irony is that we are inherently aware of the state of perfection but prefer to pretend to be ignorant of this fact.

We inherently know the state of perfection because almost all of us are blessed with a religion and it's *Book of Holy Scriptures*. The Holy Scriptures have emphasised on one eternal truth which is, *every human being is capable of attaining the state of perfection.* It is in everyone's capacity to *be all that she/he can be.*

One way or the other, we may have turned over some of the pages of this holy book carelessly. It might have crossed our minds that the state of perfection mentioned in the book is not for us but for the others. We might not have shown much interest to absorb the wisdom that is alive in the book. We might have simply ignored it and taken refuge in fictions, myths, stories and legends, while living an *utopian* dream. Suddenly we do not find any meaning in our lives. There is no purpose for our lives. Nothing is perfect. Everything is messy. We begin to question ourselves. And we begin to seek answers to our inner queries. Then and there begins our journey to perfection.

CHAPTER 1

The 7 Pure Human Desires

"Perform your prescribed duty, for action is better than inaction.
A man cannot even maintain his physical body without work."
(The Bhagavad Gita 3:8)

All human beings have 7 fundamental desires. These are their pure desires which become their life purposes. These desires propel them on the path of action. A human life is meant for fulfilling right desires through right actions. Some of these desires are quite basic and common across all the strata of society. These basic desires are entirely humane while other higher desires are associated with the noblest pursuits of a human life. These noble desires are associated with evolved personalities and persons having refined supreme qualities.

Whatever may be the nature, a desire becomes a life purpose for most of us. These desires are our inspirations to live. Fulfilment of these desires, one by one as life goes on, is what makes us satisfied and content with our lives.

The 7 fundamental pure desires that a person can have in a life time are,

1. Desire to fulfil basic physiological (bodily) needs such as food, water, clothing, and shelter. This desire is essential for self preservation.
2. Desire to have independence in career and finance related matters. This desire is fulfilled through finding a stable but well-paid career.
3. Desire to experience full range of emotions (emotional needs). This desire is satisfied through marriage and starting a family, and also through other intimate relationships such as friendships.
4. Desire to experience pure love in all relationships.

1

5. Desire to have personal power; to be a 'leader' in the society (esteem needs). This desire is fulfilled when we rise to prominent, prestigious leadership positions; when we are heard, and respected by our community members.
6. Desire to have creative imagination, intuitive abilities and insight into life (spiritual needs). This desire is normally satisfied in our creative pursuits.
7. Desire to become a perfect human being, one who is respected and venerated by all.

Now let us accommodate these 7 desires, one by one, in a 7-tier pyramid according to the degree of superiority and/or nobility of the desires.

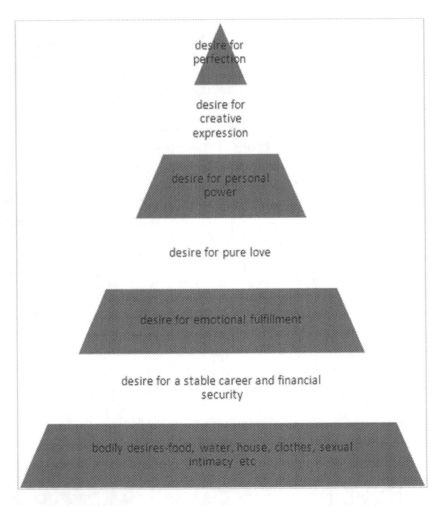

As seen in the above figure, lower level human desires are placed at the bottom of the pyramid and much nobler desires are placed towards the top. Perfection is the ultimate destination of this *'bottom-up'* journey. Natural human tendency is to follow the path of perfection by taking the *'bottom-up'* approach. We were taught one or the other point in time that this *'bottom-up'* approach is the safest and the most convenient path to perfection. Now the question is, whether one life time is sufficient to reach the point of personal perfection?

What is 'Bottom-Up' Approach to Perfection?

'Bottom-Up' approach is actually an *'Out-In'* approach. In this approach to perfection, we begin with what we have in the outside (physical) world. Much later in life, we realise the importance of our 'inner world'.

In *'Bottom-Up'* approach we begin with our material possessions and worldly attachments. Our motto is to *'work with what we have'*. Here our primary focus is to increase life's comforts, luxuries, financial security, and material possessions as well as to enhance life-enriching experiences and relationships. This human tendency to focus on wealth accumulation and self-centred life is found among all levels of people.

General human psychology is to *'follow the masses'* and we follow others blindly without even realising that where this procession is headed to. Gradually, we end up with focusing all our energy on lower level desires.

Finally, we come to realize the folly of our deeds and begin to seek a path inward. We begin self-questioning and searching for answers to our queries such as 'Who am I?', 'Why am I here?' etc.

Irony of Human Life

The irony of a human life is that not all of us are fortunate enough to satisfy all the 7 desires in a life time; but some of us are. For these fortunate few, one life time is more than sufficient to rise to the level where all their pure desires are satisfied through a productive and creative life. Different adjectives that are attributed to these few fortunate personalities are 'successful', 'perfect', 'powerful', 'influential' and 'wholesome'. They are admired and respected by the entire humanity. Some of us even worship them as our role models, dreaming that one day we can also emulate their success.

What is the secret behind their success? What do they have which we do not have? Have you ever wondered? In the following chapters, let us find out the answers.

CHAPTER 2

Perfection and Perfect Living

"For indeed the Kingdom of God is within you." (Luke 17:21)

The truth is most of the world's successful people have actually taken a different route to perfection. Instead of a *'bottom-up'* approach to fulfil all their desires, they rather tried a different approach, an *'up-bottom'* approach to perfection as shown below:

desire for perfection

desire for creative expression

desire for personal power

desire for pure love

desire for emotional fulfillment

desire for financial security

bodily desires

What is 'Up-Bottom' Approach to Perfection?

The 'Up-Bottom' approach is actually an '*In-Out*' approach. Here we begin with our '*inner world*'. We focus on '*knowing self*' to realize our inherent potential before embarking upon the pursuit of our life goals.

According to the Christian Scriptures the state of perfection is the state of full expression of *supreme energy* that is latent within us. And the unmanifested field of supreme energy is referred as '*the Kingdom of God*' in the Holy Bible. The Kingdom of God is the seat of *pure creative potential.*

Supreme energy is the source of our creative intelligence. This is the source of all our potentialities and capabilities. Access to this powerful energy source is what makes us powerful, productive and creative. That is why Jesus Christ taught us that 'seeking the Kingdom of God' should be our first and foremost life purpose. "*But seek first the Kingdom of God, and all things shall be added unto you.*" (Luke 12:31). This is the philosophy behind the art of perfect living.

In fact, the purpose of all the Holy Scriptures in the world is to show us the path that leads to a perfect life. A life of perfection can be achieved only when we focus on the full manifestation of our inherent supreme energy. In order to achieve this life purpose, conscious and constant efforts are needed in the right direction with great determination and persistence.

CHAPTER 3

Four Purposes of a Human Life

'Where there is no vision, people perish'. (Proverbs 29:18).

Any or all of the seven pure desires form the basis of a life purpose of a person. If a person has no purpose in life that person perishes while being alive. When people have a purpose to live, they prosper. In other words, a life purpose is required for every person in order to experience a life of prosperity and abundance.

For people having no resources, satisfying their hunger becomes a pursuit of life. While people of moderate means aspire for a house and for them, purchasing a house becomes a life purpose. Still further on the higher level, people aspire for higher education and a good employment. This human tendency to aspire for higher pursuits of life goes on until they feel happy and at peace with their self.

According to the Sacred Hindu Scriptures, there can be 4 purposes for a human life depending on the nature and development of that person. These are *kama* (desire), *artha* (wealth), *dharma* (duty) and *moksha* (perfection). Our pure desires fall one or the other category of these purposes. We always have a choice to decide what should be the pursuit of our life.

Majority of the great sages and philosophers of the ancient as well as the modern times believe that perfection (*be all that you can be*) is the noblest life purpose of them all. Again, the pursuit of a life purpose by a person depends upon the growth of that person in all three dimensions, i.e. physical, mental and spiritual.

Desire for Perfection is an Inborn Instinct

As Maharishi Mahesh Yogi, the proponent of transcendental meditation technique says,

> *"Consciousness is the basis of all life and the field of all possibilities. Its nature is to expand and unfold its full potential. The impulse to evolve is thus inherent in the very nature of life".*

When we look around we observe different types of people based on their age, race, religion, nationality, social status, financial status, education etc. There are poor people who are stuck in lower level of existence, always worrying about meeting their survival needs like food, water and clothing. There are people who have sufficient means to meet their survival needs but always worried about the security of their family. There are wealthy, high class people who are more oriented towards the pursuit of pleasure. They may be different in many ways but one common characteristic that prevails across the spectrum is that none of them are satisfied with their lives. Every one of them craves for something greater perhaps, perfection the noblest purpose of life. The reality of human life is that the intense desire for perfection comes to every human being quite naturally as we are God's children.

As the first chapter of the first book of the Holy Bible says,

> *"And God said, Let us make man in our image, after our likeness . . .*
> *In the image of God created He him, male and female created He them."*
> (Genesis 1:26-27).

What does it say? *We are like God.* There is only one God. Believe it. And we all, irrespective of our age, race, gender, nationality, social status, and financial status, are *His* mirror images, the living replicas of God. An image is a reflection. If a person is an image of God, that person is also a reflection of God.

God, by nature, is perfect. It means that we all are inherently capable of reflecting the perfect qualities of God; we all are capable of becoming all that we can be.

CHAPTER 4

The 7 Perfect Universal Laws

"The law of the Lord is perfect, converting the soul:
the testimony of the Lord is sure, making wise the simple.
"(Psalm 19:7)

God is perfect and the perfection of God is manifested in the Universe through the 7 powerful universal principles, *the 7 Perfect Laws.*

God is the *'Lord Almighty'*. One of the meanings of the word 'Lord' is 'the principle'. 'Almighty' means 'all-powerful'. The Lord Almighty is the powerful principle behind the creation of the Universe. The Lord Almighty is the supreme energy principle that pervades through the entire Universe. *He* rules and regulates the Universe through the 7 Perfect Laws.

The working of the Lord Almighty is beyond the grasp of even the cleverest and the most intelligent of the human beings. One of the most intelligent scientists the world has ever seen, the great Albert Einstein once said, *"I want to capture God's thoughts; rest are details"*.

If one wants to understand what is God and who is God, she/ he needs to know the perfect qualities of God. According to the Holy Scriptures, fundamental qualities of the Lord Almighty are *omniscient, omnipotent, omnipresent, omnispirit,* and *immutable.*

- Omniscient means God is the source of eternal knowledge, wisdom and goodness. *He* is the *Infinite Intelligence.*
- God is omnipotent as *He* is the source of all creation. *He* is the *Creator.*
- Omnipresent means God is all-pervading, present everywhere.
- God is omnispirit, the formless *Cosmic Spirit (the Cosmic Mind).*
- God is immutable, the changeless principle, the *Immortal.*

As mentioned above, the perfect qualities of the Lord Almighty are manifested in all *His* creation through the 7 Perfect Laws. These laws are,

1. Law of Oneness: The Lord Almighty is the source of all creation and *He* pervades through the entire creation
2. Law of Correspondence: Since the Lord Almighty is manifested in the Universe both as '*matter*' and '*energy*', there is a spiritual (mental) plane of existence corresponding to every physical plane of existence
3. Law of Vibration: The Lord Almighty pervades through the entire creation as *energy vibrations*
4. Law of Duality: The Lord Almighty expresses itself in the entire creation in *dual forms* which are polar opposites of each other
5. Law of Rhythms: The Lord Almighty rules the Universe in perfect order and rhythm
6. Law of Cause and Effect: The Lord Almighty is the principle behind every cause and effect in the Universe
7. Law of Gender: The Lord Almighty is the culmination of both masculine and feminine principles

The Law of Oneness in Detail

The first divine principle behind the manifestation of the Universe states that everything in the Universe originates from one Cosmic Spirit. All creations are interconnected. Everything in the Universe is *the supreme energy* manifested in different forms.

The entire Universe is one single unit. The energy that is vibrating through the whole universe and manifesting itself in various forms is one and the same i.e. *the supreme god energy*. Ancient Sanskrit prayer, *Vasudhaiva Kutumbakam* (Hindu Scripture, Mahopanishad VI: 71-73) reflects this truth. The meaning of this prayer is '*the whole world is one single family*'.

Law of Oneness is Law of One Cosmic Mind: According to various Holy Scriptures, a single mental principle (cosmic mind or universal soul) is behind the manifested and the unmanifested creation. In Sanskrit, this single mental principle or cosmic mind is called *Vishwatma* (the Soul of the Universe). *Vishwatma* is the supreme energy that pervades through the entire creation.

Law of Oneness is Law of Perpetual Transmutation of Energy: Everything is energy, the Supreme Energy, which is immutable and immortal. This energy is manifested in the Universe both as energy and matter. World renowned physicist Albert Einstein stated that *'energy can neither be created nor destroyed'*. Energy can only be *transmuted* into different forms. Einstein came forth with the formula **e=mc²** to prove that energy and matter are interchangeable. In this formulae, 'e=mc²', E is energy, M is mass and C is the speed of light; thus energy equals the amount of mass multiplied by the speed of light squared. What happens in the Universe is perpetual transmutation of *'supreme energy'* from one form into another form. That is why law of oneness is also law of perpetual transmutation of energy.

According to this first and the foremost divine principle, human beings are also made up of matter and energy. Our body mainly consists of different types of matter. Our mind and spirit are made up of subtle energy principles. Our thoughts, emotions, speech, and physical activities are all different forms of energy transactions. That is why there is a need for us to understand the fundamental divine laws that had gone behind our creation.

When we understand these principles of creation, we can manage our life in a better manner and we can start living a perfect life. The knowledge that the spirit of God is the living force in all of us makes us live an enlightened life. Even if we are different in many ways our essence is the same at the spirit level.

The Law of Correspondence in Detail

According to this second divine principle there exists a mental (spiritual) plane corresponding to every physical plane of existence. *As above so below. As below so above.* The *supreme energy* can be manifested in a human body just as it is manifested in the Universe. That is why this principle is also called *'the Law of Microcosm and Macrocosm'*.

Macrocosm is *the Universe* that is operative through seven mighty divine laws and microcosm is a human body with its seven mighty life force centers. In *Sanskrit* language, the life force centers in a human body are called *chakras*.

As in the Universe so in the human body. As *the Cosmic Life Force* (Cosmic Spirit) is manifested in the Universe through the seven mighty principles, individual spirit (human life force) is manifested through the seven life force centers in the human body. Yes, our body is the temple of the spirit.

As Saint Paul, an apostle of Christ says,

"Don't you know that your body is the temple of the Holy Spirit, who lives in you and who was given to you by God?" (1 Corinthians 6:19).

As per the perfect Law of Correspondence, every person has got an individual mind (individual soul) as corresponding to 'Cosmic Mind' (Cosmic Soul). As cosmic energy is manifested in the entire Universe through the workings of cosmic mind, an individual person becomes fully alive and energetic through the workings of her/his own individual mind.

It is believed that an individual mind can exist in two planes, an existence at a lower plane (lower mind) and at a higher plane (higher mind). Higher mind is considered as the seat of the spirit (soul). Lower mind is always concerned with worldly (bodily) existence while higher mind is concerned with higher purposes of life.

Perfection is a state where lower mind (existence in bodily plane) rises up to be at 'one' with the higher mind. Attuning to the higher mind enables us to strengthen our conscience and will power.

Conscience is the knowledge of right (good) and wrong (evil). Conscience is our inner voice, the inherent divine wisdom. We all have been blessed with an inherent human conscience. As we progress along the path of perfection, our conscience is strengthened by the core values that we integrate into our personality.

Will power is the judicious use of free will. Will power is the power of higher mind. That is, will power is mind power. This self-originating, self-sustaining and self-renewing mind power is the creative force in a human being. Will power is the secret behind a forceful personality and a powerful character.

So the beginning point of a perfect life is *awareness about one's own body and mind (spirit)* and to know how to tap the potential of our divine gifts of conscience and free will.

The Law of Vibration in Detail

The third divine principle which states that every creation in the Universe is in motion. Every creation is made up of energy and energy is always in motion. Energy travels in the Universe in definite vibratory patterns. This means that everything in the Universe is in motion and everything vibrates.

Law of Vibration Is Law of Change: Nothing rests; everything resonates while sending out and/or receiving energy. Everything changes either positively or negatively according to the nature of the energy exchange. In other words, change may be progressive (positive) or regressive (negative).

In the universal scenario, progressive energy vibrations such as peace, cooperation, harmony, love, and truth bring positive changes while regressive energy vibrations such as oppression, hatred, jealousy, and war bring negative changes. So, as a nation at the large level, and as a person at the individual level, we always have a choice to choose between positive and negative changes. Remember, *change is a fundamental law of life* and no one can avoid it. However, we have the power of free will to choose the nature of change that we wish to see in our life.

Change in a positive direction is necessary for growth and progress. Let us contemplate on the metamorphosis process of a butterfly. A butterfly lays egg and egg hatches into a caterpillar which, in due time, hibernates in a cocoon in order to become a beautiful butterfly just like its mother. Every person secretly aspires to be like this butterfly, to grow into a beautiful person. This aspiration is natural because growth is the basic law of the nature.

Similarly, let us also contemplate about a newly constructed water-filled pond. With time, if cleaning is not done, the water gets polluted and it starts smelling. Do any of us aspire to be like this pond? Answer is, *'definitely not'*.

In a nutshell, change is growth. Growth is life. Stagnation means there is no life at all. Have you ever wondered why you are here on the earth, living a human life? We all are here for only one purpose, to grow and to evolve into superior, perfect human beings. Only those who are able to manage change will ultimately emerge as successful and perfect.

As Charles Darwin, renowned English naturalist says,

> *"It is not the strongest or the most intelligent who will survive but those who can best manage change."*

Law of Vibration Is Law of Attraction: Like Energy Attracts Like Energy. Similar energy vibrations resonate with each other and have a natural tendency to attract each other. Sometimes this attraction and bringing together of people of same energy resonance is for the attainment of a specific life purpose. Same principle is applied in attracting perfect living conditions in our life. Our pure desires are our intentions, our life purposes. Our pure intentions are intense energy vibrations. When these vibrations are focused single-mindedly on attaining the intention, it gets manifested in our lives without much delay.

The Law of Duality in Detail

This is the fourth divine principle which states that *same energy principle has dual expressions.* There exists a polar opposite to each energy vibration. Everything in the universe has two sides (poles). There is black (absorption of 7 fundamental colours) against white (reflection of all 7 colours). There are seven deadly sins (*pride, envy, anger, sloth, greed, gluttony,* and *lust*) against seven cardinal virtues (*humility, kindness, patience, diligence, charity, self control,* and *chastity*). Some other examples are good and evil, right and wrong, failure and success, night and day, sadness and happiness, pain and pleasure, love and hatred, faith and fear, yin and yang and so on.

Venerated Christian saint Francis of Assisi captured the essence of this divine law in the following prayer:

> *"Lord, make me an instrument of your peace; Where there is hatred, let me sow love; Where there is injury, pardon; Where there is doubt, faith; Where there is despair, hope; Where there is darkness, light; Where there is sadness, joy. O Divine Master, grant that I may not so much seek; To be consoled as to console; To be understood as to understand; To be loved as to love; For it is in giving that we receive; It is in pardoning that we are pardoned; And it is in dying that, we are born to eternal life."*

Law of duality is also called as the law of relativity because dual expressions of the same energy principle are relative to each other. Good and evil, knowledge and ignorance, faith and fear, pleasure and pain, and light and darkness; all are relative concepts. For example, without light, darkness cannot be explained. Without ignorance, can knowledge be there? If night is not there, how can we appreciate day?

It is said that darkness is absence of light and ignorance is absence of knowledge. When we bring light into a room of darkness, the entire room lightens. When we introduce knowledge to a mass of ignorant people, the entire group becomes knowledgeable. Light shines in the darkness and knowledge illuminates the ignorant. For the moon to rise, the sun needs to set. Without the one, we would not have the other.

Similarly, when it comes to the battle of human life, if we did not experience sadness we would not know how to experience joy. Without pain, we would not have pleasure. This is the duality of human life. All these dual principles work together for the greater good.

We need to rejoice in the duality of our human nature. Both good and evil are a part of us. Both God and Devil reside in us at the same time. God is our goodness and Devil is our evil.

God alone is perfect. And it is a long way ahead for us to reach the point of perfection. None of us are born perfect. We are with full of human weaknesses. Having these weaknesses makes us human and overcoming these weaknesses makes us divine. While moving along the path of perfection, let us rejoice in our weaknesses. Let us rejoice in being human. Let us rejoice in overcoming our weaknesses.

Being human is the essence of a human life. Being human allows us to experience all the emotions that only a human being can experience. Our life is meant to experience both negative and positive emotions. Negative emotions are destructive and afflictive while positive emotions are constructive. While experiencing these two opposite spectrum of emotions, we know the actual effect of an emotion on our psyche. No one wants to be destroyed by own afflictive emotions. So we gradually learn to release negative emotions slowly but with full awareness so that we should never be trapped by them again. At the same time we learn to cultivate life-enriching positive emotions. By using our free will judiciously, we learn to rejoice in duality of life.

The Law of Rhythm in Detail

This is the fifth divine principle which states that *energy circulates in the universe in perfect rhythmic cycles.* The secret behind the periodic occurrences of events in the Universe is the divine law of rhythms. There is a measured flow (periodic interval) behind each event that is happening in the Universe.

Every seed has a germination cycle. A seed grows into a plant, and the plant produces seeds. These seeds are again used to grow plants of the same kind. Each plant has a life cycle and it dies after completing its life cycle. In water cycle, water evaporates into the air and then comes down again as rains.

Every plant and animal on the earth has a life span. Similarly, every event in the Universe happens in a measured rhythmic cycle at specific periodic intervals. A lunar cycle is completed in 28 days and after that a new cycle begins. 24 hours is there in a day. 365 days forms a year. In a nutshell, everything in the Universe happens in a cycle with distinct timings. There is a divine order to every creation.

As the Holy Bible says,

"There is a time for everything under heaven."(Ecclesiastes 3:7).

Every energy form in the Universe operates by rhythm, period and balance. The sun rises and sets every day. The night is followed by the day. Hence the law of rhythm is also called the law of periodicity or the law of cyclic existence.

The essence of the cyclic existence is the circular motion of the energy. This is applicable to the existence of human beings also. The cyclic existence of a human spirit is mentioned in many ancient Hindu and Buddhist Scriptures. The only difference is, in case of human beings, by virtue of the spirit bestowed upon us at the time of creation, we are capable of putting an end to our cyclic existence; for this, we need to use our free will judiciously.

The Law of Cause and Effect in Detail

This is the sixth divine principle which states that every cause in the Universe has its effect, and every effect has a cause. *There are no accidents. There are no coincidences.* An action produces a result. No actions, no results. It is as simple as that.

We need to define what we want. We need to put in our time, energy, and effort to get what we want. An action in the same direction is required to produce desired results. For digging a well, one has to keep on digging the same ground persistently until water is seen. In other words, a persistent positive action produces a positive result. Persistence leads to success. Similarly, a negative action produces a negative result.

As you sow, so shall you reap. A grower sows just a few kilograms of seeds in order to harvest hundred tonnes of the seeds of the same kind. If hard work is sown then success is reaped. If love is sown then love is harvested in manifolds. In a nutshell, according to the Law of Cause and Effect, what is given away will come back in manifolds.

In case of human beings, a positive mind (spirit) is able to sow positive thoughts which grow into positive actions and later, at the right time, positive results are harvested. On the contrary, a negative mind spreads negativity everywhere. Negative people carry negative vibes around. We need to avoid negative people in all situations in order to protect ourselves from their negativity because energy transfers from one medium to another. If we associate ourselves with negative people we tend to absorb their negativity. Similarly, if we keep company with good people, we also get transformed by their positive energy.

The Law of Cause and Effect also implies that everything in our life is happening according to a divine plan. If we observe our life closely we can see that nothing in this life is accidental or unexpected. It is actually God's own plan which is at work. So believe that whatever happens in our life is happening according to a divine plan. And we are bestowed with a 'free will' to choose the right attitude towards our life's events.

The Law of Gender in Detail

This is the seventh divine principle which is about sacred feminine and masculine. It states that *there are both male and female energy principles behind all creation.* Everything in the Universe exists in pairs; exists as male and female. When all male qualities are manifested in a male, we call it 'sacred masculine' and when all female qualities are manifested in a female, we call it 'sacred feminine'. In order to create something, male and female principles must come together. As we can see, both in animal and plant kingdoms, male and female principles need to come together for reproduction and multiplication.

Male and Female Energies of God: God created us as male and female. As the Holy Bible says,

"In the image of God created He him, male and female created He them." (Genesis 1:27).

God's male energies are manifested in male species of his creation and *His* female energies are manifested in female species. Male and female may be different and opposite to each other in many ways but they are equal. Both male and female energies are needed in equal measures for sustaining the equilibrium in the Universe. For every male, a compatible female is created. When there is compatibility in the union of male and female energies, perfection is the result.

Masculine and Feminine Qualities: A male is born with dominant male energy principles which are called masculine qualities. Major masculine qualities are courage, strength, faith, fortitude, self control, persistence, truth, honesty, straightforwardness, independence, and risk-taking behavior. A female is born with dominant female energy principles which are called feminine qualities. Major feminine qualities are humility, gentleness, modesty, meekness, compassion, kindness, charity, serenity, sensitivity, love, forgiveness and joy.

The beauty of a human being is that there is no other creation in the Universe which is blessed with the *power of choice*. A man can choose to express his feminine side by developing all feminine qualities that is inherent in him in addition to the full expression of all his manly qualities. Best example is, Jesus Christ. Similarly, a woman can develop all her manly qualities that are inherent within her in addition to the expression of all her feminine qualities. Best example is Joan of Arc of France.

According to the world renowned astrologist and numerologist Linda Goodman, there is a little man in every woman and a little woman in every man. It is perfectly natural and desirable for an evolved man to express feminine qualities such as gentleness, compassion, meekness and sensitivity. Similarly, it is perfectly natural for an evolved woman to show manly qualities such as courage and independence.

Evolved and empowered women are a powerful presence in the society. An evolved woman is capable of becoming a strong, positive change in the society. Considering this, Linda Goodman once remarked *"The Queen must sit on her throne beside the King if there is ever to be Peace in the Kingdom"*. Therefore, in all areas of life a woman should be treated at par with her male counterparts.

Respect for Women: Both males and females are the images of God. If a male is capable of becoming a 'perfect' person, so is a female. Perfect life is where a woman is respected by her man and treated fairly in all dealings. When the lady of the house is happy, content and treated with respect, she expresses all her feminine qualities naturally and her feminity becomes the joy of the household. Equal measures of male and female energies must be blended together for experiencing perfection in life.

It is often said that there is a woman behind every man's success. If there is a woman behind every man's success, there may be a man behind every woman's success. If a woman can supplement the energy principles that are lacking in a man, the same is true in case of a man. A man can supplement the energy principles that are lacking in a woman. It is always just perfect when a compatible man and woman come together for the right cause. That is why it is so blissful to be in a right relationship— whether it is marriage or friendship or any other intimate relationship. Who does not want to be in a good marriage? Who does not want to be kissed and hugged by spouse? Who does not want to feel the ecstasy of an intimate love? Right relationships fulfill all the emotional needs of a person; most importantly the need for *love*, the universal emotional need. Love is so wonderful and blissful that miracles happen in every moment of life.

A woman is inherently full of *'female God principles'*. Every woman having incorruptible purity is a divine feminine, a goddess in her own terms. Feminity is nothing but full manifestation of divine feminine principles in a woman. Only a feminine woman is able to discover the masculinity latent within her. A woman needs to cultivate her feminine principles to the full manifestation before she starts to develop her masculine qualities latent within her. Similarly, a man is inherently full of *'male God principles'*. A man with an incorruptible masculinity is a divine masculine, a God in his own terms. A progressive society is one where men and women are equally respected, and accepted for what they are and who they are.

CHAPTER 5

Personal Perfection

"Then the Lord God took some soil from the ground and formed a man out of it; he breathed life-giving breath into his nostrils and the man began to live."
(Genesis 2:7)

The Lord God created a living human being from two components, soil (*body*) and life-giving breath (*life force or spirit*). The individual spirit which is limited in a human body is a part of the Lord God who is *Infinite Spirit* and *Infinite Intelligence* by nature. In our body dwells God's spirit.

A Sufi proverb goes like this, *"I searched for God and found only myself. I searched for myself and found only God"*. In other words, one's search for perfection begins with oneself, precisely speaking, in the realm of her/his body.

Since the spirit is the life-giving force in a human body and this spirit comes from God, all human beings are connected at the spiritual level. This is the essence of the law of oneness in the plane of human existence.

We have both physical (body) and spiritual existence (mind or spirit) at the same time. In other words, human beings exist in full compliance with the law of correspondence.

According to the law of vibration, the life-giving force of a human being, the individual spirit, is expressed in a human body as subtle energy vibrations.

According to the law of duality supreme energy has two expressions, matter and energy. In a human being, physical body is made of gross matter while spiritual body is made of highly subtle supreme energy. Physical body is the seat of 'individual ego' while spiritual body (etheric body) is the seat of 'individual spirit'. In a human body, 'ego' and 'spirit' are always in conflicts. This is the secret behind the duality of a human life.

According to the law of rhythms, the Universe with all its life forms is a cyclic existence with distinct life stages. This is applicable to human beings too. A human being has a definite life span and after that she/he dies. As the Holy Bible says,

> *"The dust returns to the earth as it was, and the spirit returns to God who gave it."* (Ecclesiastes 12:7)

Law of Rhythm is also expressed in a human body in its metabolic functions. For example, beating of the heart, inhalation and exhalation cycles of breathing, and pulse movements; all these processes occur at definite intervals.

Law of cause and effect governs the entire range of human actions. If a person needs to get desired results she/he needs to act in that direction. Law of gender is also manifested in the creation of human beings. For every man, there is a compatible woman.

5 Laws of Personal Perfection

1. Every person is called to a life of perfection
2. Perfection in a person is the epitome of the perfection in the Universe
3. As perfection is expressed in the Universe through the 7 perfect principles, perfection is expressed in a person through the 7 life force centers. Life force center is the seat of the supreme qualities of the spirit, therefore the seat of the personal power
4. Perfection is not an overnight phenomenon. It happens slowly and steadily as the person goes through various life defining experiences at different stages of her/his life
5. Personal perfection denotes the highest stage of personal development

CHAPTER 6

Life Force in a Human Body

*"A living body is not merely an integration of limbs and flesh
but it is the abode of the soul which potentially has perfect perception,
perfect knowledge, perfect power and perfect bliss."*
Saint Mahavira, Jainism

Even though we are of body and spirit, our natural tendency is to identify ourselves with our body, its health, beauty, and appearance. Most often, we forget that in our body dwells a *spirit* too. In fact *the Spirit* is the essence of a human life. *The Spirit* is the part that comes from God. Since God is perfect in nature and it's *His* own life-force that forms our Spirit, we also have the potential to become perfect. For this, we need to learn to attune our body to the spirit within. The spirit is the seat of our mental principles—*lower mind* and *higher mind*. Perfection is state of existence at the higher level of mind and this will happen only when we learn to attune our body to our higher mind.

The Supreme Energy is the Life Force in Our Etheric Body: Our body is everything. It has two components, physical body and spiritual (etheric) body. Spiritual body is the seat of both our lower mind (generally termed as 'mind') and higher mind (generally termed as 'spirit'). Hence broadly speaking, we exist in three dimensions—physical, mental and spiritual. Our essence is a combination of all these three—*Body, Mind* and *Spirit*. A perfect living addresses our existence at all these three levels. Therefore, *a perfect living is a life style choice that focuses on bodily health, mental health and spiritual health with equal importance.*

A perfect living begins with the proper care of body. A healthy mind and spirit is found only in a healthy, disease-free body. Therefore it is our primary duty to take care of our body through proper diet and physical exercise. This fact is reflected in the words of the renowned Hindu sage

Adi Shankara Acharya. As he says, *"Knowing that I am different from the body I need not neglect the body. It is a vehicle that I use to transact with the world. It is the temple which houses the pure self within."*

Isn't it obvious that body is the vehicle of the individual spirit, and the spirit is the perfection principle in a human being?

Life Force Centers

The life force or the power of the spirit in a human body is expressed through 7 life force centers (*chakras*) of the etheric body. Each *chakra* has its respective location in the physical body which is associated with a particular organ system and glands.

Life Force Center 1: The lowest and densest of the life force centers, root *(Mooladhara)* Chakra is located at the base of the spine corresponding to the organ system of kidneys and adrenal glands. The sensory organ associated with this chakra is nose and sense associated is smell. The root chakra or the base chakra is associated with basic survival needs like food, water, clothing and shelter. This is the seat of crude energy which is primitive, untrained, unregulated and unripe form of energy which gets transformed into refined, regulated and ripe form of pure energy as it moves along the upper chakras and finally reaches at the crown chakra. The elemental principle associated with this life force center is earth. The gem stone vibration that is in resonance with root chakra is coral. Color energy vibration that is associated with root chakra is red.

Life Force Center 2: Sacral *(Svadhisthana)* Chakra is located just above the base chakra at the lower abdominal region corresponding to the reproductive system of body and gonads (ovaries or testicles). The sensory organ associated is tongue and the sense is taste. This chakra is associated with our security and financial needs such as basic comforts of life and a stable career. The elemental energy associated with this chakra is water. The gem stone vibration that is in resonance with sacral chakra is amethyst. Color energy vibration that is associated with sacral chakra is orange.

Life Force Center 3: Solar Plexus *(Manipura)* Chakra is in the region of upper abdomen corresponding to liver and pancreas. The sensory organ associated is eyes and the sense is sight. This chakra is associated with our emotional needs. The elemental energy associated with this chakra is fire. The gem stone vibration that is in resonance with solar plexus chakra is emerald. Color energy vibration that is associated with solar plexus chakra is yellow.

Significance of Lower Three Chakras: The three life force centers situated below our heart center corresponds to low frequency energy vibrations associated with our gross desires (survival, security and emotional needs). Our gross desires are our basic human tendencies. When we move beyond the realm of these lower life force centers, we begin to express our divine tendencies. A human being is both human and divine. Our human nature and associated human desires are expressed through the lower three life force centers. Similarly, our divine nature and associated divine qualities are expressed through the higher life force centers.

Life Force Center 4: Heart (*Anahata*) Chakra is located in the chest region just above the heart and the gland associated is thymus. The sensory organ associated is skin and sense is touch. This chakra is associated with our need to experience pure love. This is the integration point between three lower chakras and three upper chakras. Lower chakras represent our basic human desires while upper chakras represent our noble aspirations. Our noble aspirations can be pursued only with a pure heart. Heart chakra is the seat of the highest form of emotional force, i.e. love. Love conquers everything, both our basic desires and noble aspirations (higher pursuits of life). The elemental energy associated with this chakra is air (wind). The gem stone vibration that is in resonance with heart chakra is ruby. Color energy vibration that is associated with heart chakra is green and/or pink.

Significance of Upper Three Chakras: Three upper chakras that are situated above our heart region are the throat chakra, the brow chakra and the crown chakra. All these chakras are associated with high frequency energy vibrations i.e. subtle, refined energies.

Life Force Center 5: Throat (*Visuddha*) Chakra is located in the throat and associated glands are thyroid and parathyroid glands. The sensory organ associated is ears and sense is hearing. This chakra is associated with our esteem needs such as need for personal power or self mastery. The elemental energy associated with this chakra is ether. The gem stone vibration that is in resonance with throat chakra is sapphire. Color energy vibration that is associated with throat chakra is blue.

Life Force Center 6: Brow (*Ajna*) Chakra is located between eye brows. It is believed that this is the seat of 'Sixth Sense'. The organ system associated is lower brain and the gland is pineal gland which when activated the person is said to possess intuitive abilities and insight. The gem stone vibration that is in resonance with brow chakra is diamond. Color energy vibration that is associated with brow chakra is indigo.

Life Force Center 7: The highest and finest of the chakra, Crown (*Sahasrara*) Chakra is located at the top of the head. It is believed to be the seat of 'Pure Wisdom' or 'Pure Consciousness'. The organ system associated is upper brain and the gland associated is pituitary gland. This chakra is associated with our need for perfection. The gem stone vibration that is in resonance with crown chakra is pearl. Color energy vibration that is associated with crown chakra is violet and/or white.

Purification of Life Force Centers

Life force at each *chakra* needs to be in its pure, pristine form for the associated glands and organ systems to function properly in the human body. More precisely speaking, pure energy at the life force centers must be maintained in its pure, uncontaminated form for a human body to function in its original, disease-free form. We all know that our body is originally meant to be disease-free. The original principle on which a human body functions is perfect health. It's our lifestyle choices that have the potential of corrupting our life force centers (*chakras)* is what result in various diseases and illnesses in our body. If we aspire for a perfect living, there is only one life principle to follow: *Purity of Life Force Centers.*

Life force contamination happens on a daily basis in our lives as we are human beings with all inherent weaknesses. We interact with different types of people and deal with different situations of life on a regular basis. Sometimes we attract other people's negative energy towards us and absorb some of it. If we do not know how to contain it, we tend to express negative aspects of the absorbed negativity. It this is the case, then our current situation becomes worse than our initial condition. Therefore it is imperative that we should know how to tackle the negative situations of our life without getting affected by it. Also, we must always replace our negative qualities with that of positive ones.

If pure life force at a *chakra* remains in its pristine form, which is highly unlikely in a human life, the entire life force at the *chakra* can be tapped by the person. Such a person inherently possesses all the supreme qualities associated with that *chakra*. For example, some of the supreme qualities associated with the *root chakra* are earthly qualities such as patience, humility, and strength. A person who has a clear, pure *root chakra* tends to possess these supreme qualities naturally.

For a perfect living, we need to understand the sources of life force contamination so that we can take immediate purification measures as soon as our life force centers are contaminated. Life force contamination at a particular *chakra* blocks the availability life force at that center thus creating permanent energy blocks. Therefore such energy blocks need to be cleared on a regular basis in order to keep our life force intact as life force is the field of all potentialities and creativities.

Practices for Purifying Life Force Centers

Purification of Root Chakra: Hobbies such as gardening and cooking (conscious food preparation); leisure time activities like walking barefoot on the earth; therapeutic practices such as aromatherapy; and practicing supreme qualities such as devotion and commitment (be in a committed relationship, or be devoted to someone or something) are recommended for purifying life force at the root chakra. This is because the element associated with the root chakra is earth. The recommended practices are intended to strengthen the earth element of the body and associated earthly qualities.

Purification of Sacral Chakra: Water-related leisure activities like walking in the rain, and walking near natural water bodies; daily routines like daily bath (hydrotherapy) or writing a daily journal (reflection on life); and practicing supreme qualities such as openness, adaptability (be adaptable to change) and emotional stability (expressing all emotions in a balanced way) are recommended for opening life force at the sacral chakra. This is because the element associated with the sacral chakra is water. The recommended practices are intended to strengthen the water element of the body and the qualities associated with water.

Purification of Solar Plexus Chakra: Early morning activities such as rising with the sun and watching sun rise and late evening activities such as watching sun set, and star gazing; sun bath and/or light therapy; learning to live a disciplined life with focus on life's goals; practicing supreme qualities such as hope, optimism, and positive attitude; practicing positive affirmations and daily prayer and candle gazing are recommended for opening life force at the solar plexus chakra. This is because the element associated with the solar plexus chakra is fire. The recommended practices are intended to strengthen the fire element of the body and the qualities associated with fire.

Purification of Heart Chakra: Walking in the fresh air, study of the Holy Scriptures, reading good books (feeding mind with good information), practicing deep, conscious breathing and practicing supreme qualities such as love, forgiveness, charity and gratitude are recommended for opening life force at the heart chakra. This is because the element associated with the heart chakra is air. The recommended practices are intended to strengthen air element of the body and the qualities associated with air.

Purification of Throat Chakra: Attuning to the sounds of nature around us, practicing chanting mantras (sacred words), practicing supreme qualities such as self discipline, truth and honesty, spending time in silence and solitude, practicing conscious speech and active listening (conscious hearing) and music therapy such as practicing any musical instrument and/or vocal music are recommended for opening life force at the throat chakra. This is because the element associated with the throat chakra is ether. Power of words, sounds, music, and silence is used to strengthen ether element of the body.

Life force at Brow Chakra and Crown Chakra can be accessed through practices such as deep meditation.

Personal Perfection through Life Force Transmutation

The life force movement from lowest to highest chakras represents the development of a human being. Concentration of life force at the base chakra means that a person's entire energy is trapped in the realm of lower existence, where the person is fully involved with the fulfilment of basic survival needs such as food, water, clothing and shelter. Similarly, the concentration of life force center at the crown chakra means that the person's entire energy has been transmuted into the pure energy vibrations and such a person is said to have achieved perfection in life.

In a nutshell, for personal perfection or full degree personality development, a person must know how to release the inherent life force that is caught trapped in the lower chakras and to make this force flow towards the higher chakras.

If the life force centers in our body are not functioning in its inherent nature, then we cannot express the inherent qualities associated with those life force centers. In such a scenario, we suffer in body (i.e. bodily diseases) as well as in spirit (i.e. issues with personal development). So it is very much essential that one needs to know about one's own body and the functioning of life force centers.

Summary

Body, Mind and Spirit

1. Body, mind and spirit are interconnected. Nothing stands alone.
2. Body (physical and spiritual) is everything. Body is the beginning point towards the journey of perfection.

Physical Body

3. Physical body is a collective system of organs and associated glands. The 7 major organ systems are the lower part of the body (base of the spine), lower abdomen (sacral), upper abdomen (solar plexus), chest region (heart), throat region, lower brain (brow) and upper brain (crown).
4. Precisely speaking, the system of glands, the endocrine system of the human body plays a significant role in the proper functioning of the physical body by regulating body's physiological and metabolic activities in a systematic manner.

Etheric (Spiritual) Body and Life Force

5. Corresponding to our physical body, we have an etheric (spiritual) body which is the seat of our life force.
6. Life force is expressed in our body through 7 life force centers.

Body and Spirit—Physical Body and Spiritual Body

7. Each life force center corresponds to each organ system in our physical body.

8. If life force at a particular life force center is pure (not contaminated), the person is able to manifest all supreme qualities associated with the life force center.

9. This also means, the corresponding organ system is at its functional best.

10. Proper care of body and its organ systems opens up life force centres and the person is able to express supreme qualities

Life Force Purification

11. If a life force is contaminated or blocked, a person may resort to external tools and practices such as prayer, meditation, practicing supreme qualities etc to purify the life force.

12. Life force purification is essential and needs to be a regular practice as a blocked life force center may result in diseases of organ system associated with that life force center.

13. A blocked life force may also mean that the person is unable to express the supreme qualities associated with that life force.

Supreme Qualities—the Personal Powers

14. Everything is interlinked—bodily functions, mental functions and spiritual (supreme) qualities—through our life force.

15. Practicing a supreme quality opens up the corresponding life force center; thus proper functioning of the corresponding organ system may be achieved.

16. Purifying a life force center by external tools and practices such as meditation and physical exercise enhances life force at the corresponding center. The result is well being of the person and she/he is able to experience and express the supreme qualities associated with the life force

17. All are practiced together. Nothing stands alone.

Nature of Human Desires Affect the Inherent Nature of Life Force

Human desires affect inherent nature of life force centers either positively or negatively. It is discussed above that each life force center is associated with a particular human desire which becomes the major life purpose for a person whose spirit is operating from that level. The relationship between life force centers and basic human desires is given below:

Life Force Center	Basic Human Desires
Root Chakra	Survival or Self Preservation—Healthy body and Stability of life; to find means to satisfy survival needs like food, water, house and clothing
Sacral Chakra	Security—Stability of career; to find financial resources to satisfy survival needs like food and water as well as security needs like basic comforts of life, financial investments etc
Solar Plexus Chakra	Emotional Health—Healthy mind and Stability of emotions; to have emotional support of family, friends and relationships
Heart Chakra	Pure Love—Balanced life based on love; To have a healthy body and mind, and to have a stable career and family life
Throat Chakra	Esteem—High self esteem, self mastery, personal power, leadership positions
Brow Chakra	Creative Expression—insight and intuitive abilities; intellectual, aesthetic and moral pursuits
Crown Chakra	Perfection

Life Purposes at Different Life Stages

According to the Hindu Scriptures, the progressive life stages of a human life are *Saisava* (infanthood), *Balya* (childhood), *Kaumara* (adolescence), *Yauvana* (youth) and *Vardhakya* (old age). Infanthood is from the time of birth to up to 2 years of age, childhood is from the age of 3 up to 12 years of age, adolescence is from 13 years of age up to 19 years, youth is from 20 years to 59 years of age and old age begins at 60 years of age.

Each life stage has a purpose to fulfil. The period of infanthood, childhood and adolescence is the period of preparation and training. As the Holy Bible says,

"Train up a child in the way he should go, even when he is old he will not depart from it." (Proverbs 22:6)

During this period, one prepares oneself to face the world, both *the world within* and *the world without.* During this period a child learns to survive in the world without getting affected by life's struggles and to perform worldly and moral duties in the best possible manner. Moral training and academic training are equally important for the children to become powerful personalities. The Holy Scriptures is the best tool for training a child in morality. As Saint Paul says,

"All Scripture is breathed out by God and profitable for teaching, for reproof, for correction, and for training in righteousness." (2 Timothy 3:16)

The purpose of youth is to create *artha* (wealth), to perform one's *dharma* (duties) and to experience *kama* (desire) in a rightful manner. This is the period of family life, wealth creation and social service. During this period, learning process reaches its peak and the individual who lived a good life senses a feeling of restlessness. With this restless feeling the individual enters the next stage of life.

Vardhakya, the old age happens to be the last stage of a person's earthly life. This is the period of retirement from active worldly life and transferring one's legacy to the next generation. The only purpose of *vardhakya* is *moksha* (personal perfection). The old age is supposed to spend in contemplation on permanent nature of God and impermanence of death.

Survival or Self Preservation as Life Purpose

Satisfactory fulfilment of survival needs is the primary criterion for a human being to live like a human. When we look around we can witness many incidences where lack of basic survival needs drive people to their basic primitive and animalistic behavior. When the bare minimum needs for self preservation is not met, people become ready even to compromise

31

on their basic human values. It is beyond doubt that self-preservation becomes the first life purpose for any living human being.

People who lack basic survival needs are always motivated by the promise of the fulfilment of these basic needs and are ready to do anything to meet these needs. Their entire life force is focused on achieving these targets—food, water and shelter.

Security as a Life Purpose

For a majority of people, major life purpose becomes the pursuit of different kinds of security—emotional security, economical security and social security. An individual's major sources of emotional security are Family (parents, siblings, spouse and children) and Friends. Economic security is the result of having a good financial status and investments. Social security is derived out of a sense of social status which is direct result of worldly achievements.

People who lack security needs are always motivated by the promise of the fulfilment of these security needs. Their entire life force is focused on achieving these targets—career progress, and good financial investments.

Duty as a Life Purpose

Once survival and security needs are fulfilled, the immediate tendency of a person is to fulfil emotional and psychological needs through a dutiful living. Such a person seeks to have meaningful relationships in intimate friendships, emotional bonding with family members and in sexual intimacy with spouse.

All these needs—survival needs, security needs and emotional needs—can be fulfilled simultaneously or in different stages depending upon the growth level of the person. But it is a proven psychological fact that even though multitudes of thoughts may occupy a human mind in a life time, only one thought dominates at a given point in time. Hence, the natural tendency of a person is to focus all life force on the realization of the single thought which is dominant at that point in time.

When dutiful living becomes a life purpose, a person's life is mainly focused on performing different types of duties in a rightful manner.

There are different types of duties such as duty to God, duty to parents and siblings, duty to spouse and children, duty to friends, relatives, neighbours and well wishers, duty to society and finally, duty to the environment. Whatever may be the nature of our duty, we must discharge our duty in a rightful manner. As the Holy Quran says,

"Be mindful of your duty, and do good works; and again, be mindful of your duty, and believe; and once again: be mindful of your duty, and do right. God loves the doers of good." (The Holy Quran 5:93)

Duty towards Society

We all have a duty towards the society in which we live. It is so easy to sit in meditation and experience *'peace within'* as compared to *'find peace'* while moving around among the suffering, downtrodden and poor people. Jesus Christ has actually taken this difficult route to perfection. While living among the people amidst their negativity he conquered their evil. Dying on the cross amidst humiliation, physical pain and mental agony, he kept peace within and prayed for his tormentors. He was still able to love them—true service is based on selfless love. Living a secluded life while avoiding all pains and discomforts, and negativities and distractions of the world, is much easier as compared to the path of service that is chosen by Jesus Christ. Path of service is not for the faint-hearted.

Higher Life Purposes

A person on the path of perfection, saving precious time and energy, is able to focus on further growth and development through self-knowledge, worldly knowledge and spiritual knowledge.

Significance of Life Force in the Pursuit of Life Purpose: Life force in its pristine form at each center allows a person to fulfil the life purposes or desires in a positive, rightful manner. However, if this desire is ego-based, the inherent negative force of ego contaminates the purity of life force and the person tries to fulfil desires in a negative, wrongful manner.

A description of ego and ego-based qualities are dealt in detail in the following chapter.

CHAPTER 7

The Supreme Qualities

"Humility, lack of hypocrisy, harmlessness, forgiveness, uprightness, purity of body and mind, steadfastness, self control, absence of egotism, non-attachment, devotion to God and perseverance in Self knowledge, all these qualities constitute wisdom"
(The Bhagavad Gita 13: 7-11)

The Supreme Energy is expressed in the human body as the Supreme Qualities. Our physical body forms our physical personality while our individual spirit is the source of our individuality or uniqueness. Our supreme qualities, which are actually natural expressions of the spirit, originate in the realm of our etheric body.

What are the supreme qualities? Supreme qualities are nothing but the expressions of the qualities of the Supreme Energy (God) that dwells within us. Supreme qualities are divine qualities. Supreme qualities are supreme virtues, by which a person is made perfect. A perfect person is a superior person. As legendary Chinese Philosopher Confucius says,

"The way of the superior person is threefold: Virtuous, they are free from anxieties; Wise, they are free from perplexities; and Bold, they are free from fear."

The Supreme Qualities

Each life force center corresponds to a particular elemental energy principle and associated qualities. For example, root chakra represent earth energy, sacral chakra water energy, solar plexus chakra fire (light) energy, heart chakra wind (air) energy and throat chakra ether (space)

energy. Brow chakra and crown chakra represents perfection, i.e. perfect combination of all these five elemental energies. These five elemental principles are called '*pancha tattvas*' or '*pancha boothas*' in Sanskrit language.

According to the Sacred Scriptures, every creation in the universe, including human beings, is composed of five elements-earth, water, fire, wind and ether. Each of these elements, being divine in origin, expresses a set of unique divine qualities or supreme qualities that are inherent in them. Earth is associated with qualities such as strength and stability; nourishing and nurturing; and giving and receiving. Water is associated with depth, transparency, sensitivity, acceptance, flexibility, and adaptability. Fire is associated with warmth, radiance, purification, and reaching out to all. Wind or air is life-giving, refreshing, rejuvenating, cleansing, and available to all. Ether is divine and reflective.

A description of five elements, corresponding life force centers and associated supreme qualities is given below.

Element	Life Force Center	Associated Supreme Qualities
Earth	Root chakra	Faith (reliability, trustworthiness) and Fortitude (strength, courage, and stability) Humility (modesty, gentleness, meekness, down-to-earth, grounded and balanced nature) Patience, Diligence and Persistence (focus and concentration, right efforts) Generosity or Charity and Gratitude (giving, nurturing and nourishing, fruit-bearing, supportive, and sustaining nature)
Water	Sacral chakra	Truth and Integrity (transparency, accountability, and authenticity) Compassion (kindness, sensitive and emotional nature, empathy) Purity of mind and cleanliness of body
Fire or Light	Solar Plexus chakra	Radiance of character or goodness of nature (purifying, rejuvenating and renewing nature) Forgiveness (ability to let go)

Wind or Air	Heart chakra	Love (reaches out to everyone irrespective of any conditions)
Ether or Space	Throat chakra	Self Control (i.e. control over everything or self mastery)

Other two chakras that are not mentioned in the above table are brow chakra and crown chakra. Life force at these centers is manifested as highest divine qualities a human being can possess.

Brow chakra is associated with supreme qualities like intuition, insight and creativity. Creativity is expressed when a human mind is fearless and at peace with itself. That is, the supreme quality associated with brow chakra is inner peace. Similarly, life force at crown chakra represents pure consciousness, pure awareness, pure knowledge and highest peak of human wisdom.

Here we have 7 sets of supreme qualities with respect to the 7 life force centers. For personal perfection, we need to master all these supreme qualities. Some of these qualities are inborn while other qualities need to be cultivated with a conscious and constant effort.

Supreme Qualities, the Life Force behind Fulfilment of Pure Desires

A supreme quality is a positive life skill that helps us to find the right path towards our life's destination (life purpose) while providing us with the sufficient life force to carry on with our journey to destination. A supreme quality is associated with the fulfilment a particular human desire, and a specific life force. In order to be successful in our life, to progress on the path of perfection, we need to cultivate these supreme qualities in us with conscious efforts.

CHAPTER 8

Core Value System

"But the Spirit produces love, joy, peace, patience, kindness,
goodness, faithfulness, humility and self-control."
(Galatians 5:22)

In the Christian Scriptures, the supreme qualities are upheld as 'the fruits of the Spirit'. These are the qualities that should form the basis of our core value system.

Our core values determine our character and our character determines our destiny. Therefore, it is very much essential for us to focus on the integration of core values into our personality.

There are 7 sets of core values with respect to the 7 chakras. A description of these core value systems and associated human desires is given below.

Core Value System	Associated Supreme Qualities	Life Force Center	Associated Human Desires
Core Value System 1	1. Faith and Fortitude 2. Humility 3. Patience, Diligence and Perseverance 4. Charity and Gratitude	Root Chakra	Healthy body and Stability of life (survival needs)

Core Value System 2	5. Truth, Compassion and Purity	Sacral Chakra	Stability of career (security needs)
Core Value System 3	6. Radiance of Character or Goodness of Nature	Solar Plexus Chakra	Healthy mind (emotional needs)
Core Value System 4	7. Love and Forgiveness	Heart Chakra	Balanced life based on love (need for love)
Core Value System 5	8. Self Control	Throat Chakra	High self esteem, self mastery, personal power (esteem needs)
Core Value System 6	9. Inner Peace and Intuition	Brow Chakra	Creativity, insight and intuitive abilities (need for creative expression)
Core Value System 7	10. Knowledge, Wisdom and Happiness	Crown Chakra	Perfection (need for enlightenment)

Each of the supreme qualities is a positive force and has a particular positive vibration. These supreme qualities, just like their source of origin i.e. *the Supreme Energy,* are universal, immutable (unchanging) and ever-lasting.

For a perfect living, a person needs to integrate these universal supreme qualities into personal value system. There are different types of values, family values, societal values, spiritual values etc. Family values may change. Societal values may change. But the spiritual values, the supreme qualities are unchangeable because these are the values (virtues) of the Spirit.

Significance of Positive Values

Our values make us aware of our limitations as a human being. The supreme qualities are our core values. These value systems should be integrated in to a person's personality for a perfect living. Our value system determines the quality of our thoughts. Since our thoughts are the beginning point of the life path that determines our destiny, it is highly imperative that we have a strong value system.

However, *'value erosion'* is the mark of today's modern society and most of our young generation does not even know what right values are. Cultures and values are different for different societies. Family values are held in high regard in traditional societies while values such as 'individualism' and 'liberalism' are held in high esteem in liberated societies. None of these values are good or bad in themselves. The only thing is, the person holding a particular set of values must know how to behave in a socially acceptable way within the limitations of those value systems. In older times, people clearly knew their values and accordingly behaved in an acceptable manner. The advent of internet and worldwide media broadcasting services, however, changed this scenario considerably. World has become a global village and everyone seems to know everything. Everyone is so eager to experience all that is being broadcast through the visual media, no matter *good* or *bad*. This is the biggest problem of today's times. People do not know what to choose. They do not know what are right values, *traditional values* or *liberal values* or *both*. They are a confused lot. They are ignorant of 'the universal, changeless, core values'. That is why this modern era is marked so prominently with an accelerating rate of value erosion, both among the youth and the adults.

Consumerism has become a fashion word and materialistic tendencies are becoming prominent which suppress the inherent spiritual tendencies of the human beings. Not only value erosion is the curse of this era but changed values also. So it is very important for all of us to go back to our roots to revisit the values upon which our spiritual legacy has been built. Now it's time for all of us to reinforce our brains with these renewed and refreshed values.

The 7 Core Value Systems in Detail

Core Value System 1

Core value system 1 comprises of qualities such as faith, fortitude, humility, patience, diligence, perseverance, generosity (charity) and gratitude. These are called earthly qualities (inherent qualities of the element earth), the fundamental qualities that enable a person to lead a comfortable worldly life in a *rightful* manner. Practicing these supreme qualities opens up life force at the root chakra.

Core Value System 2

Core value system 2 comprises of qualities such as truth and integrity, compassion and purity. These are inherent qualities of the element water. These are the qualities required for a person to progress in career or professional life. Practicing these supreme qualities opens up life force at the sacral chakra.

Core Value System 3

Core value system 3 comprises of qualities such as goodness and forgiveness. These are the inherent qualities of element fire or light. Practicing forgiveness and good deeds opens up life force at the solar plexus chakra. These qualities are required for a person to form stable relationships and friendships. Goodness of nature and forgiveness are the keys to excellent networking skills.

Core Value System 4

Core value system 4 comprises of quality of pure love. This is the inherent quality of element air (wind). We need air to breath. Air is what makes our body alive and functional. In the same way, love is what makes our mind alive and functional. Love is the connecting link between a person's earthly (worldly) pursuits and creative pursuits. Love opens life force at the heart chakra and the person is able to express the quality of pure love. Love is beginning point for the higher pursuits of life.

Core Value System 5

Core value system 5 comprises of quality of self control (self regulation). The inherent quality of the element ether or space is that it is self-regulating. Will power is the force behind self control. Practicing self control opens up life force at the throat chakra. Self control is required by a person to progress into the realm of self mastery. Self mastery is the secret behind personal power (charismatic personality).

Core Value System 6

Core value system 6 comprises of quality of inner peace. Practicing inner peace opens up life force at brow chakra. This is the seat of accurate perception and intuition. This quality is required by a person who aspires for deep insights into human life and mysteries of the universe. Opening up brow chakra opens the creative intelligence within us. We become creative and productive.

Core Value System 7

Core value system 7 comprises of quality of knowledge and wisdom. Pure knowledge and pure wisdom is pure consciousness itself. Pure consciousness is what makes a person 'enlightened' or perfect. This is the highest form of evolvement of a human life. This is what each of us should be aspiring for.

Spirit-based Positive Values and Ego-based Negative Values

Our body is the seat of both ego and spirit, two opposing energy principles. It is said that human birth is divine and a new born baby is the symbol of divinity manifested. That is, a human life begins in a state of purity. Gradually, as the child goes through the dualities of the human life, it either becomes strong in spirit or weak depending upon its basic temperament.

Three basic temperaments of a human being, according to Vedanta philosophy, are *tamas*, *rajas* and *sattva*. *Tamas* is ignorance or darkness; *Rajas* is desire and action; and *Sattva* is poise, calmness, and contemplation. Our journey towards perfection begins with the basic temperament with which we are born. Most of us express a combination of all three temperaments.

Since perfection is our life purpose, our journey must be from *tamas* to *rajas* to *sattva* to *trans-sattva*. Trans-sattva stage is called the state of perfection. This is the hidden wisdom contained in the following prayer:

> "*Asado ma sat gamaya* (lead us from the unreal to the real);
> *Tamso ma jyotir gamaya* (lead us from darkness to light);
> *Mrtyor ma amrtam gamaya* (lead us from mortality to immortality)."

We may be sceptical that one life time may not be sufficient for us to reach the state of perfection. Who knows! Perhaps for some of us one life time may be more than sufficient to become *perfect superior human beings*.

Ego and Ego-based Qualities

Ego is expressed in a human body as ego-based qualities and spirit is expressed as spiritual qualities. Since the spirit is the source of origin of core values, these values are positive energy vibrations (positive forces). Similarly, ego-based values are the source of negative energy vibrations. 'Ego' is the major human weakness that prevents a person to rise to the level of perfection. In fact, all personal weaknesses are by-products of a person's ego. Our personal weaknesses are our vices (non-virtues). These are the contaminants of our 'pure' spirit.

In other words, all major contaminants of the spirit are the direct offsprings of ego. And there are seven offsprings of ego and these are, *pride, lust, anger, greed, laziness, jealousy,* and *covetousness*. In Christian Scriptures, these are called seven cardinal sins. These are the seven inner demons that exist in every human being in varying degrees. According to the Buddhist philosophy, *ego* gives rise to 10 major non-virtues. These are *killing, stealing, sexual misconduct, divisive talk, telling lies, harsh speech, senseless chatter, covetousness, harmful intent,* and *wrong views*.

Every religion in the world advocates against committing a non-virtuous action. Still human nature is so weak that there is no dearth of non-virtuous actions committed on the earth. Every non-virtuous action brings with it an evil effect of an equal measure to the act committed. This happens in compliance with the universal law of cause and effect. The Holy Scriptures of all religions strictly prohibit committing any of the non-virtuous actions.

As Nagarjuna, an ancient Hindu sage says,

"One who is born as a human and then becomes involved in ill deeds is even more foolish than one who fills with vomit a gold vessel adorned with jewels."

However, some religions particularly Buddhism advocate that the bad effect of a non-virtuous action can be mitigated in four ways—*by disclosing it, by regretting having done it, by intending not to do it in the future* and *by engaging in virtuous actions such as public (social or community) service.*

Existence in Lower Plane vs. Existence in Higher Plane

Human nature in its lower plane of existence is purely ego-based. In an ordinary human life what happens is that as life progresses, we let the spirit (original state) be contaminated by focusing on the satisfaction of our ego-based needs only. Ego gets satisfied at the disposal of inherent *supreme energy* within us. When there is always a withdrawal from the inherent positive energy, balance is always negative. This negative human state allows ego and its offsprings to breed at the cost of the spirit thus concealing the true essence of a human existence. When we are not aware of our true nature any more, the only thing that matters most is our 'Ego'.

As the Holy Bhagawad Gita says,

"Under the influence of false-ego one thinks himself to be the doer of all activities while in reality all activities are carried out by nature as natural process." (Bhagawad Gita 3:27).

When ego is the only thing that matters us most, we are lost in the realm of worldly desires. We are incapable of releasing the potential of our inherent supreme energy. Ego not only blocks the life force center but makes it contaminated and corrupted also. Swami Brahmdev, a prominent Indian sage thus summarizes the concept of ego:

'Ego eats a lot of energy. To maintain your ego, a lot of energy is needed. Without ego, you start feeling light—ego is like a big burden which you are carrying; when you are walking carrying a heavy burden, automatically you will get tired very fast. And with no ego, you feel light; you don't feel tired with that.'

Isn't it so amusing to know that *the spirit* and *the ego*, or *the good* and *the evil*, or *god* and *devil* inhabit in the same human body. That is why it is so often said that there is a dark side to every human being just as there is a good side.

Ego vs. Spirit: Dual Principle of a Human Life

Positive and negative forces cannot occupy a body at the same time. One cannot serve *the Spirit* and *the Ego* at the same time. One or the other must dominate. All people who are successful at the art of perfect living are well aware of this truth.

As the Holy Bible says,

> *"No one can serve two masters, for either he will hate the one and love the other, or he will be devoted to the one and despise the other."* (Matthew 6:24)

According to the law of duality, for each positive value there exists an equal but opposite negative value. In our body, 'the Spirit' is always in conflict with 'the Ego'. This is the secret behind the 'duality of human existence'—*an existence in a lower plane (ego-based) versus an existence in a higher plane (spirit-based).*

In an ordinary human life, the ego is always manifested more and the manifestation of the individual spirit is suppressed up to some extent. As God's children, our life purpose is to travel from this lower plane of existence to a much higher plane of existence.

As the renowned scientist Albert Einstein says,

> *"A human being is a part of a whole, called by us 'universe', a part limited in time and space. He experiences himself, his thoughts and feelings as something separated from the rest . . . a kind of optical delusion of his consciousness. This delusion is a kind of prison for us, restricting us to our personal desires and to affection for a few persons nearest to us. Our task must be to free ourselves from this prison by widening our circle of compassion to embrace all living creatures and the whole of nature in its beauty."*

For people like us who aspire for a perfect living, personal perfection is gained, steadily but slowly, with every step that we take in our life. This perfection is achieved as we progress along the journey of life fulfilling our instinctual urges (basic rightful drives and desires), at the same time evolving into better versions of our previous selves. The force to move ahead in life comes from our core value systems. This is the significance of conscious cultivation of positive core value systems in our life while resisting the temptation of absorbing the negative values from our surroundings.

Negative Values vs. Positive Values

Some of the prominent negative values that are found across the entire spectrum of the society are, pride, arrogance, egocentricity, conceit, vanity (vainglory), anger, gluttony, greed, covetousness, lust, attachment, possessiveness, inferiority, depression, despair, indifference, judgment, anxiety, resentment, indecision, self-pity, guilt, disbelief, doubt, fear, revenge, justification, withholding (inability to let go), rejection, disappointment, defiance, resistance, submission, and sacrifice. Ego-based negative values are the sources of our vices or sins. Our negative values are the reasons behind blocked life force.

As Saint John, apostle of Jesus Christ says,

"Aversion, anger, accusation, hatred, resentment, and pride obstruct the work of the Holy Spirit." (1 John 3: 14-17).

Persons of negative values are full of negative vibrations. Their vices or sins are the source of negative vibrations (negative forces) for themselves as well as for others. People having negative value systems are the force of evil in a society. So there is a need to create awareness among the young generation about the right values. There is a need to persuade people to integrate a core value system of positive values into their personality. A description of positive core values and their opposite negative values is given below:

Positive Values	Negative Values
Knowledge And Wisdom	Ignorance
Inner Peace	Restlessness, Worry, Anxiety, Stress
Faith	Fear, Doubt
Hope	Despair
Optimism	Pessimism
Positive Attitude	Negative Attitude
Diligence	Laziness (Sloth)
Open-Minded	Close-Minded
Acceptance	Rejection

Forthrightness, Straightforwardness	Cunningness, Shrewdness
Honesty	Dishonesty
Responsibility	Irresponsibility
Devotion (Faithfulness)	Unfaithfulness
Love	Hate, Indifference
Forgiveness	Resentment, Revenge
Self Control	Sense Indulgence
Patience	Impatience, Anger
Compassion	Ruthlessness, Cruelty
Gratitude	Ingratitude
Charity	Greed
Renunciation	Possessiveness
Non-Judgment	Judgmental, Critical, Fault-Finding, Slander, Calumny
Purity Of Body, Cleanness	Unclean
Humility, Modesty, Gentleness	Pride, Ego, Vanity, Conceit, Vainglory
Detachment	Attachment
Non-Covetousness	Covetousness
Non-Violence	Violence
Kind Speech	Harsh Speech
Temperance	Gluttony
Non-Injury, Harmlessness	Injury, Harmful Intent, Harmful Views
Lack Of Hypocrisy	Hypocrisy
Constructive Criticism	Destructive Criticism
Truth-speaking	Telling lies

Strength of Positive Values

Our core value system is the foundation of our personality. A personality built upon the core values is the strongest personality and such a person has the strongest of all powers, i.e. personal power (personal magnetism). In other words, personal values and virtues are the source of a person's strength, character (personal quality), charisma and uniqueness. Values determine a person's actions and beliefs. Values secure a person's life path by helping to choose the spiritual values over ego-bound desires. A person having a core value system will never compromise on quality of life because that person is disciplined, mentally tough, resilient, sensitive and vulnerable. The foundation on which a person's core value system rests is *Faith in the Spirit*. This is the secret behind a strong character. The secret behind a perfect personality is strength of character, which is built on a strong foundation of core values.

A perfect person is embodiment of all virtues. Such a person is powerful and the source of this power is goodness, the power of virtues. A perfect person is like a bright sun shining in the sky. Such people carry the light of their goodness wherever they go. All who come near them are attracted by their personality and strength of character. At least some people look at them as role models and learn from them and in the process they also get transformed for the better.

As the Holy Bhagavad Gita says,

> "*The mode of goodness being purer than the others, is illuminating, and it frees one from all sinful reactions. Those situated in that mode develop knowledge, but they become conditioned by the concept of happiness.*" (The Holy Bhagavad Gita 14: 6)

Changed Values

Science and technology are advancing at a fast pace, triggering knowledge penetration in multi-dimensions. With the faster penetration of knowledge at all levels of society, societal values are changing. People should be very much aware of these changed values so that they can adapt their core values to the changed environment, without compromising on the essence of the values. In order to make it possible one should keep on strengthening the core values by paying close attention to its application in day to day life.

CHAPTER 9

The 7 Personal Powers

"But those who hope in the Lord will renew their strength.
They will soar on wings like eagles; they will run and not grow weary,
they will walk and not be faint."(Isaiah 40:31)

The 7 Core Value Systems are the 7 Personal Powers. Perfect living is powerful living. A perfect person is powerful and has tremendous energy at disposal. Their strength comes from the power of their supreme personal qualities. Their core value systems are the source of their personal power.

The 7 personal powers are,

1. Power of Faith, Fortitude, Humility, Patience, Diligence, Perseverance, Generosity (Charity) and Gratitude—the power that help us to withstand life's struggles
2. Power of Truth, Compassion and Purity—the power that help us to live a fearless life
3. Power of Goodness—the power that help us to make right decisions which is beneficial for ourselves and others
4. Power of Love and Forgiveness—the power that help us to spread our light and goodness all around us
5. Power of Self Control (Self Mastery)—the power that gives us mental poise not to overreact even in extreme provocation
6. Power of Inner Peace and Intuition—the power the gives us our creative intelligence; the source of our creativity
7. Power of Knowledge, Wisdom and Happiness—the power that helps us to respond accurately to life's situations after due assessment

First three personal powers help us to lead a successful worldly life. Success in worldly life leaves us with sufficient time to contemplate on the mysteries of life. We gradually realize that whatever we have achieved or done so far has only a superficial meaning and we crave for the experience of pure love. Once we are beyond the realm of pure love i.e. after acquiring the ability to give and receive the pure love, we naturally progress towards a higher level of existence. The powers that help us to progress towards our ultimate destination are the power of self mastery, inner peace and wisdom.

In other words, the 7 personal powers encompass all three aspects of a human existence—body, mind and spirit. If we want to be perfect then our body, mind and spirit should work as a single unit. Our understanding about our bodily needs such as balanced diet, sleep and exercise compels us to focus on these areas and thus we are able to keep ourselves in perfect physical health. Our understanding about the needs for mental development such as education, reading, and social interactions helps us to focus on these areas. We can achieve a state of spiritual health through practicing meditation, yoga, religion, and religious rituals.

Wrong Lifestyle Choices—A Hindrance to Perfect Living

If we aspire for a perfect living then we need to avoid these three scenarios,

1. Focusing only on body while neglecting mind and spirit
2. Focusing only on mind while neglecting bodily and spiritual needs
3. Focusing only on spirituality while denying the needs of body and mind

In fact, we all are bound by duty to our creator to aim for perfection. A perfect living is a purposeful living. A purposeful life is not wasted in the realms of unhealthy emotions and feelings. A purposeful living seeks its own destiny. A perfect living is possible only for perfect persons. A perfect living is meant for a fully-developed person. A perfect person is like the brightest star in a star-filled sky. Unfortunately there are very few people who are perfect among us. However, the truth is that we all have the potential to become perfect persons if we put conscious effort towards that direction. Now is time for us to be perfect, *just perfect.*

CHAPTER 10

Personal Power System 1

"Everything is possible to those who believe." (Matthew 9:23)

Personal Power System 1 comprises of Power of Faith and Fortitude; Power of Humility; Power of Patience, Diligence and Perseverance; and Power of Charity and Gratitude.

Power of Faith and Fortitude

Definition of Faith

"Faith is the substance of things to be hoped for, the evidence of things that appear not." (Hebrews 11:1).

Faith is the beginning point of a journey that leads to a fulfilled life. Greatest of all American Presidents, Abraham Lincoln once said, *"To believe in the things you can see and touch is no belief at all; but to believe in the unseen is a triumph and a blessing."*

Faith is like a seed sown in the field which when watered and nurtured grows into a seedling, later into a healthy plant which bears good quality fruits. Faith in God should be inculcated in a child by its parents at a tender age. As the child passes through different growing stages, it holds this faith in God so strongly that nothing can stray the child from the right life path.

Our success is determined by the size of our faith. Fear is the root cause of every failure and therefore it is necessary to destroy fear by developing faith.

Faith Results in Hope and Optimism

Faith results in hope and optimism. According to Christian Scriptures, hope is a strong and confident expectation about the future and/or the successful outcome of something.

If we have a strong faith, we have a strong value system. If we have a strong value system, we have a strong decision-making ability. Decision-making is easy when we know clearly what our values are and how to behave within the limits of our value systems. Knowledge and assurance of our own values instils confidence in us to make right decisions and right life choices.

There are two groups of people around us. First group of people are full of positive forces, happiness, energy, confidence and faith; we call them charismatic people, people with personal power. They are like magnets. Wherever they go, they attract people and people want to be with them. While second group of people are full of negative forces, fears, complaints, anxieties and doubts. They are so repulsive that nobody wants to be associated with them. When we see the charismatic people with full of attractiveness, vitality and happiness, we secretly wish to be like them. The truth is, every human being has an inherent potential to become a highly magnetic and charismatic person. It is every person's birth right to live a *'fully alive'* life. To be fully alive, we need to do only one thing, *believe in God and believe in Self.* People having personal power are the highly successful people in life. The beginning point of a perfect living is nothing but *faith*—Faith in God and Faith in Self.

Faith Conquers Fear

Faith is the opposite of fear. Faith is fearlessness. Our life's purpose of perfection can be pursued only if we have sufficient faith to overcome our *'fear of unknown'*. There are different kinds of fear, fear of rejection, fear of accidents, fear of death, fear of illnesses etc. These fears are our inner demons. When we conquer these fears one by one, we conquer all our inner demons and we are free to pursue the path of perfection.

Fortitude—the Power of Resilience

Faith leads to fortitude. *Fortitude is the power of resilience*. Fortitude refers to a person's courage to face life's struggles boldly. Fortitude is manifested in a person as the power of resilience and the ability to let go of negative emotions. Fortitude enables us to move out of our comfort zones and face the realities of the life boldly. Fortitude believes in 'fight' rather than in 'flight'.

Fortitude—the Power of Repentance

Fortitude may also refer to *a person's courage for repentance*. In the arena of life, we all are like infants who are eager to learn how to walk. It falls down and then gets up to walk again and falls down again. This *'falling down and getting up'* cycle continues until it learns how to walk perfectly and its legs get sufficient strength to support its body. The beauty of repentance is in the fact that it makes us stronger individuals and helps us overcome our previous weaknesses. In Christian Scriptures, Judas Iscariot is portrayed as 'the evil betrayer' and he was damned to a life in hell through his suicide. Actually there are two betrayers of Jesus Christ in the Holy Bible—Peter and Judas. Peter promised Jesus that he would never deny him, come whatever may. But during Christ's accusation trials, Peter denied firmly, that too to a slave girl, being ever associated with Christ, to protect his own life. Later Peter was glorified as 'the Head of Christ's Church' just because he had the strength to admit his mistake and repent it. He overcame his weaknesses through the power of fortitude and was blessed with a life with Christ in eternity. What made this big difference, a life in hell for one and a life in heaven (eternity) for another; the courage to admit one's weaknesses, the courage to repent, and the nobility to correct the mistakes.

Fortitude—the Power of Authenticity

Fortitude is the courage to be unique, authentic and original. The highest form of courage is the courage to be oneself, the courage to be original. There are two types of courage, physical courage and moral courage. The source of moral courage is mental strength. One needs moral courage to speak truth, to be honest, to be fair and just, and to resist temptation.

Fortitude—the Power of Risk-taking

Fortitude is the courage of risk-taking with prudence. Risk-taking is moving out of the comfort zone to venture into the world of impossibilities. If we do not have sufficient courage to accept risks, we will never realize our full potential. We will never do all that is there for us to do. We will never become all that we can be. We will never experience real beauty, joy and freedom.

Fortitude—the Power of Openness and Curiosity

Fortitude is the courage to be open-minded. Perfection belongs to the people, who have child-like qualities. There are many child-like qualities that we can assimilate in our personality such as openness, innocence, energy, enthusiasm, joy, spontaneity, trust, truthfulness, playfulness, generosity, and curiosity.

As Jesus Christ says in the Gospel of Saint Luke,

"Let the children come to me, and do not hinder them, for to such belongs the Kingdom of God. Truly, I say to you, whoever does not receive the Kingdom of God like a child shall not enter it."(Luke 18:17).

Openness is the quality that treats and accepts other persons with all their human weaknesses. Openness opens a channel of empathy between two souls. Openness is straightforward in speech and actions. Openness is forthright in attitude. Openness also means openness to new experiences, ideas, and arguments. It is a quality characterized by lack of pretentions, and a deep attention to inner feelings. Openness is also deeply rooted in intellectual curiosity. Renowned scientist Albert Einstein once stated, *"The important thing is not to stop questioning. Curiosity has its own reason for existing."*

An open-minded person is free of prejudices and biases. Openness is a quality of liberated people. Open-minded people are unconventional, unbiased, non-judgmental and with liberal views on life. In reality, we all crave for openness and the freedom of expression comes along with it. However we simply cannot do it just because we follow conventional rules and widely chosen path of comforts. It is deeply rooted in our nature to stick to our familiar routines and stay within our comfort zones rather than exploring the world around us to gain new experiences and thereby gaining new insights into the self-evident principles of the Universe. We are not using all our intelligence. We prefer a small, simple life with a narrow range of interests rather than letting ourselves open to new experiences.

Child-like qualities like openness and curiosity are desirable only when these qualities are associated with the power of discretion. Power of discretion (prudence) is the quality that enables us to make right life choices. The world in which we live is a highly sophisticated and complicated world. To live a good life in this world, we need to be wise as serpents and at the same time innocent as doves.

As Jesus Christ says in the Gospel of Saint Matthew,

> *"Behold, I am sending you out as sheep in the midst of wolves, so be wise as serpents and innocent as doves."* (Matthew 10:16).

Fortitude—the Power of Faithfulness and Commitment

Fortitude is the courage to be committed, devoted, faithful and loyal. Faithfulness is the quality of being worthy of another person's complete trust and confidence. Faithfulness is being loyal to a person; and being reliable and trustworthy. Faithfulness is actually a commitment to fulfil the trust that other persons place in us. The most important characteristic that the most successful men in the world share in common is *faithfulness in their relationships.*

There are different kinds of relationships; intimate relationships of married couples; relationships between parents and children; relationships between brothers and sisters; social relationships with the community members; relationships with the elders and the teachers; and friendships.

Faithfulness in a Marriage

Marriage is a sacred bond. It is the union of two different individuals with two different kinds of energies (coming together of male and female energies). In a married relationship, couples needs to focus on each other's growth and happiness before anything else.

As the first book of the Holy Bible says,

"Therefore shall a man leave his father and his mother, and shall cleave unto his wife: and they shall be one flesh." (Genesis 2:24).

In a married relationship, there needs to be mutual understanding, love, trust and respect between the couples. Most importantly, both of the couples need to feel physically safe and emotionally secure in their marriage. The physical, mental, intellectual and spiritual compatibility between the couples is a sure way to success in marriage. In modern liberated societies people prefer a companion who is equally educated and career-oriented. Education and dedication to a career helps a person to cultivate mind. Mind cultivation leads to emotional intelligence. Emotionally intelligent couples are able to understand each other's emotions perfectly and to modify their behaviour accordingly.

In a marriage, a couple needs to be spiritually compatible. Mystic poet Kahlil Gibran has captured the essence of spiritual compatibility of a married couple in a poem in a very beautiful way.

The poem goes like this,

"You were born together and together you shall be for evermore; You shall be together when the white wings of death scatter your days; Aye, you shall be together even in the silent memory of God; But let there be spaces in your togetherness; And let the winds of the heavens dance between you."

Spiritual compatibility between the couples is an important criterion for a successful married life. They are committed to respect their marriage and respect each other's personal space and freedom. When there is mutual respect in a relationship, that relationship has a long shelf life and it works wonders for the growth and development of the couple. Such relationships are meant for nurturing, sharing and creating the goodness within us. Marriage or friendship or any other relationship is definitely not a license to encroach into one another's personal space.

It is a common knowledge that in many of our traditional societies, women are not treated at par with their husbands in their married relationships. The Holy Scriptures say that a wife is an equal partner in a married life and a husband needs to honor his wife, and show understanding in all phases of their life together.

As Saint Peter, apostle of Christ says,

> *"In the same way, you husbands must give honor to your wives. Treat your wife with understanding as you live together. She may be weaker than you are, but she is your equal partner in God's gift of new life."* (1 Peter 3:7).

Sexuality in Marriage

Sexual energy is the most important energy of a human body. A married couple needs to have a healthy sexual life. Physical intimacy is a basic bodily need which is to be fulfilled in a healthy manner. In physical union, not only two bodies are merged into one but two souls also. This soul union is the spiritual side of a physical union. That is, sexual activity is not just a physical activity; it has a psychological and spiritual side also. During sexual activity, our endocrine system is highly active involving a variety of hormones such as oxytocin (love hormone or anti-stress hormone), dopamine (happiness hormone), and endorphins (endogenous hormones that create a sense of well being). Oxytocin induces characteristics such as strong pair-bonding and connection, sense of curiosity and learning, and positive feelings. When dopamine is involved in adequate levels in a human body, the person feels happy, motivated, and has a good feeling towards others. There are actually some family experts who prescribe healing energy associated with a healthy sexual life as a remedy for all family-related problems. In a healthy physical union, focus is on 'giving' oneself fully to each other. It is a completely selfless activity and is purely based on love for each other.

As Saint Paul says,

> *"Let the husband render to his wife the affection due her, and likewise also the wife to her husband. The wife does not have authority over her own body, but the husband does. And likewise the husband does not have authority over his own body, but the wife does. Do not deprive one another except with consent for a time, which you may give yourselves to fasting and prayer; and come together again so that Satan does not tempt you because of your lack of self-control."* (1 Corinthians 7:1-40).

Faithfulness in Friendships

Friendship is a relationship based on mutual affection, and faithfulness. Friendship is one of the strongest forms of interpersonal bonds. True friendship is possible only between similar-minded people. It is said that a friend in need is a friend indeed. Having a single trustworthy friend is better than having a thousand acquaintances. Having a closely-knit circle of friends is even better.

As the Holy Bible says,

"A person standing alone can be attacked and defeated, but two can stand back-to-back and conquer. Three are even better, for a triple-braided cord is not easily broken."(Ecclesiastes 4:12).

Similarly it is said that 'old is gold'. An old friend is a golden friend. Reliability of an old friend increases with time. *"Never abandon an old friend; you'll never find a new one who can take his place. Friendship is like wine, it gets better as it grows older."* (Sirach 9:10)

Faithfulness in Social Relationships

"So whatever you wish that others would do to you, do also to them, for this is the Law and the Prophets." (Matthew 7:12).

This is the 'Golden Rule' of the Holy Bible and the secret behind successful relationship management. *Treat others with respect and be respected.* We can teach people how to treat us. That is, it is us who teach others to treat us in a particular way by either actively rewarding or passively allowing their particular mode of behavior towards us. In any situation of our life it is always wise to 'reflect' and 'respond' than to 'react' and 'regret'.

The art of perfect living carefully avoids all those actions and circumstances that bring regrets and negativity in a life. It avoids harsh speech and actions.

As Saint Paul says,

"Never speak harshly to an older man, but appeal to him respectfully as you would to your own father. Talk to younger men as you would to

your own brothers. Treat older women as you would your mother, and treat younger women with all purity as you would your own sisters. Take care of any widow who has no one else to care for her." (1 Timothy 5:1-3)

In a social scenario, good communication skills and interpersonal skills are important for good relationship building process. For improving our communication skills, we need to make communication a top priority in all relationship areas of life. An important criterion that is needed for successful communication is openness. Be open-minded and receptive to people. This creates a receptive environment for communication whether it is verbal or non-verbal communication. Medium of verbal communication is speaking, writing and listening while non-verbal communication is achieved through eye contact, smile, gestures and body language.

A strong network of healthy relationships is actually one of the important ingredients of a perfect life. Interpersonal skills help us in building long lasting relationships. Empathy is the strongest foundation of a successful interpersonal skill set. Empathy is the quality that expresses genuine interest in others, particularly in their sufferings with the motive of alleviating their pain and suffering. Empathy allows one to perceive things from the other person's point of view.

While building healthy social relationships we need to avoid the habits of hypocrisy and negative criticism. These are two worst enemies that stand in the way of successful social relationships. Hypocrisy and negative criticism are the characteristics of weak people. Weak people will always complain about life, no matter how much goodness life brings to them. They will always blame other people and circumstances for their weaknesses. In a married relationship, if a husband is weak, he will always blame his wife for his inefficiencies and failures. If it is a wife who is weak she will always nag about her husband's deficiencies. There is only one remedy for such situations, '*the Golden Rule*'.

Power of Humility

"*Blessed are the meek, for they shall inherit the earth.*" (Matthew 5:5).

Humility is absence of pride. Humility represents modesty, meekness and gentleness of behavior. Humility is a state of being humble, and selfless. Other virtues associated with the value of humility are respect for others, dignity of manners, and politeness. Humility demonstrates the strength of character and a value-based upbringing. It is said that pride goes before fall but humility brings honour.

As Saint James says,

> *"Humble yourselves before the Lord, and he will exalt you."* (James 4:10).

Humility is Realistic Estimation of Self Worth: According to the renowned English writer Clive Staples Lewis, *"Humility is not thinking less of yourself, it's thinking of yourself less."* Humility is our ability to estimate our merits and demerits at its true worth. That is, humility is the realistic estimation of self worth. Humility believes in giving respect and commanding respect. Best example of humility is Jesus Christ. He is selfless, fearless, modest, authoritative and authentic.

Humility is expressed in Authenticity and Originality of Nature: Humility is a person's strong reliance on own authentic nature. Humble persons accept everything in their life with an attitude of gratitude towards God. They know that the source of all goodness is God.

Humility Believes in Correcting Mistakes: Humility is the ability to handle mistakes, complaints, and criticisms positively and constructively. Humility allows a person to admit own mistakes, to correct them and to learn from them. A humble person will never make same mistake again. Humility allows a person to face all complaints in a calm spirit and to take corrective measures for the common benefit.

Power of Patience, Diligence and Persistence

> *"Everything that happens in this world happens at the time God chooses."* (Ecclesiastes 3:7).

Patience is the Ability to wait for the Right Time by Enduring Everything without Getting Angry. Patience is a virtue that believes in the divine law of rhythms. There is a right time for everything. But it does not mean that we need to wait patiently without doing anything. Preparation or training is essential to get desired results after a period of patient waiting.

Significance of Training

"A ship, which is not well prepared, in the ocean, goes to destruction together with its goods and merchants. But when a ship is well prepared, and well joined together, then it does not break up, and all the goods get to the other shore." (Dhammapada, the Hindu Scriptures).

An old adage goes like this, *"luck is when preparation meets opportunity."* For the pursuit of perfection, patience is very much needed. Preparation or training at all three levels—physical, mental (intellectual) and spiritual—is the secret behind a perfect life.

As Sama Veda, the Hindu Scriptures says on training,

"The one who is well armed for the battle of life possesses good qualities, become successful and prosperous. Such a person experiences real happiness."

Majority of us were fortunate enough to have supportive parents, teachers and peers. They helped us to prepare to face the world boldly. They helped us to find the right path. Now it is our responsibility to guide the young generation and show them the right path. Every new born child is a gift to the humanity. Every child has immense potential to become a great human being. But the child has to go through right life-defining experiences. A child's training begins at home. Parents are its role models. A child's brain is like a sponge. It absorbs everything from its surroundings. So it is important that a child should be brought up in a good environment. After the initial training at home, the child has to go through right academic and moral education to develop its brain and mind. Spiritual training on core value system is as important as academic training. According to Christian theology, the moral values and religious teachings are seeded into a child's mind from its time of birth to the age of 7 years. These years are crucial in a child's holistic development and parents need to pay close attention to their children's development during these years. While training children, give them challenges. Learn to say 'No' to them. Do not corrupt them. Introduce spirituality and moral values while they are young. Also give them good advices.

Not every person can be trained on the path of perfection. A person who can perfectly be trained has qualities such as a desire to learn, listening skills, ability to reflect, ability to reject false views, and truth-orientation.

In today's modern world, young generation is being saturated by a flood of immoral and sexually explicit materials from a variety of audio-visual media. If they are not educated on right moral values at a very young age, it becomes very difficult for them to focus on what is really important in later stages of their life. Parents and teachers are highly responsible for the moral development of a child. Inculcating right values in the children should begin from their very young age, and then only they will grow up into strong decent human beings with right values. People having right values are always respected in the society as *'having values means having decency and strength'*.

Value erosion is the mark of modern world. There are very few role models now who show the future generation the right direction. What today's young generation needs is not advanced technologies and hi-fi electronic gadgets. They need right role models. Role models, who can inspire them, motivate them and show them the right path and the right direction.

Let us all try to be better role models for our young generation. Let us show them what matters most through our actions. *Actions speak louder than words*. Let them see our actions and believe in our spirit. *Seeing is believing*.

Patience is Angerlessness

"A fool gives full vent to his anger, but a wise man remains in control." (Proverbs 29:11).

Almost all the Scriptures categorize anger as the prominent characteristic of a fool. A foolish person is ever ready to get angry even without a cause.

An Arabian proverb goes like this,

"A fool may be known by six things, anger without cause, speech without profit, change without progress, inquiry without object, putting trust in a stranger, and mistaking foes for friends."

According to M K Gandhi, India's national father and a saintly figure, patience is angerlessness. It is not easy to practice angerlessness in all life situations. It requires constant practice and conscious efforts.

As Gandhi says,

"It is not that I do not get angry. I don't give vent to my anger. I cultivate the quality of patience as angerlessness, and generally speaking, I succeed. But I only control my anger when it comes. Control comes with constant practice."

5 Laws of Anger Management

1. Refuse to be provoked by external circumstances, by negative people and by toxic relations. *Practice self-control*
2. Practice controlling anger whenever you get provoked by using following techniques
   a. Count one to ten and ten to one
   b. Ask yourself a few questions—'Should I be controlled by this person/this external circumstance?', 'Is it really worth it?' etc
3. Share your anger with someone you trust in case you got angry and are in an emotionally disturbed state
4. You can share your anger either with a close family member or friends. Make sure the person is trustworthy so that you can pour it out to that person without inhibition. After sharing the distress, soon forget it. If you have dearth of people whom you can trust, go to your personal space (meditation room, prayer room, library etc) and sit in silence and solitude, sharing all of it with your God. Open your heart to Him and ask Him to unburden it.
5. Be angry within control. Get angry if your 'getting angry' brings positive results. *Getting angry in a controlled way (anger within your control) with the people who deserve your anger but for the right reason and the right cause, and for getting right results is an art.*

Patience is the Result of Self Control

Patience is a byproduct of self control. Control requires constant practice. *Practice makes man perfect.* Patience is a byproduct of humility and generosity as well. That is, patience is not a fundamental virtue like love and peace; instead it is the result of having a set of right fundamental values such as self-control, humility and generosity. Patience requires self control not to complain about any discomforts and to tolerate all adverse situations. Patience requires magnanimity of heart to allow others to go ahead while waiting for the right time. Patience requires humility to stand alone and to stay unnoticed in adversities.

Patience Requires Power of Discretion

Though patience believes that there is a right time for everything, a person must use power of discretion to exercise the virtue of patience. Sometimes, *'slow and steady wins the race'* attitude may work wonders. But other times, *'just do it'* attitude is highly important, especially in some critical situations.

Diligence

Diligence is absence of sloth or laziness. Diligence believes in the dignity of work. According to the Christian Scriptures, sloth (laziness) is a cardinal sin, a non-virtuous action. It is said that *an idle mind is Devil's workshop.*

Diligence Leads to the Art of Honest Work: We all believe in work. We were taught that *hard work is the key to success.* Hard work is honest, smart work; a work done with full integrity. When a work is done with a devoted mind it becomes our worship. Remember the old adage, *work is worship.* In ancient Hindu Scriptures, one can find *karma yoga* as one of the purposes of a human life. *Karma yoga* is nothing but seeking God in our work just as we seek God in our prayers and meditations (i.e. *Bhakti Yoga,* 'Bhakti' means 'devotion to God').

We all have a birth right to lead an abundant life which lacks nothing. The key to this abundant life is honest work. Diligence is the value that propels us on the path of action. There is nothing beautiful in poverty. Poverty is the result of laziness and inaction. In fact, poverty is a social evil. Crime breeds when people desire for higher needs that they are unable to meet with their limited resources. The only solution to such situations is eradicating poverty through employment generation and empowering people through education.

Employment or work is the major financial source for most of us; therefore we all need to believe in honest work; we need to do our work, however small it is, with a great pride. Work makes a person financially self-reliant. And this self reliance instils a great sense of self respect in a person.

5 Laws of Honest Work

1. Find a work that you love and then work with love and honesty.
2. Be proud of what you are, however small your work is.
3. Believe in quality of work rather than quantity.
4. Incorporate a service mentality in your work. We serve the Universe through our work.
5. Be excellent at what you do. *Wealth follows excellence.*

The Art of Honest Work is the Art of Excellence

"Therefore by their fruits you will know them." (Matthew 7:20)

Excellence is a quality where one works with love, takes pride in work, and pays attention to details. It is said that the quality of labour reflects the maker's character. The art of excellence is gaining expertise in a specialized field of study such as cooking, gardening, dance, acting, writing, music, musical instruments, photography etc. It is not possible for a human being to know everything about everything. It is said that a *master of all is a master of none.* But it is possible to know everything about a particular subject. Specialized knowledge that is accumulated through formal academic training, life experiences and observations is of great value in attracting a successful life.

Knowledge is power when it is organized and intelligently used for the benefit of the mankind. At the same time, foolishly used little knowledge is a dangerous thing. A Burmese proverb goes like this, *"A man with little learning is like the frog who thinks its puddle a great sea."*

Values of Patience and Diligence
Leads to the Art of Perseverance

Perseverance is the ability to focus all of our energy in the right direction continuously and patiently until desired results are obtained.

The values of patience and diligence are the building blocks of the art of perseverance. Perseverance or persistence is also called 'bulldog tenacity', a fundamental success habit. Persistence can only be achieved by will power. When we have 'perfection' as our life's purpose and we aim for its achievement through a definite plan, then persistence becomes the key to success. Persistence is a quality which is based on definiteness of purpose, desire for its attainment, self sufficiency (independence), specialized knowledge, and the power of diligence and patience.

Perseverance is Steadfastness

"And let steadfastness have its full effect, that you may be perfect and complete, lacking in nothing." (James 1:4).

Perseverance is right efforts in the right direction. The beginning point is definiteness of purpose. There is no turning back once life's purpose is established. We must persist on the attainment of the life purpose.

As the Holy Bible says,

"Anyone starts to plough and then keeps looking back is of no use to the 'Kingdom of God'." (Luke 9:62).

Perseverance is the secret behind success, prosperity and abundance. The quality of persistence is in resonance with the universal law of action. We reap what we have sown.

Perseverance is the Art of Focus and Concentration

Perseverance is the life skill that enables us to focus all our energy on our life purpose. Focus means concentrating our full force on a single purpose with the intent to realize it, i.e. focus is concentrated energy which is powerful. When we focus our concentration on a single purpose, our mind is fully present with that purpose. All scattered energy, both physical and mental, is brought together to the point of focus which accelerates action in the right direction. That is, single-minded focus on a purpose is necessary for its successful attainment.

The Art of Unitasking

Unitasking is the result of increased focus and concentration. Unitasking is the ability to concentrate at a single task at hand without any distractions and mental conflicts. There is holiness in unitasking because in unitasking we completely merge ourselves with the task by giving all our attention and focus essential for its quick completion. It is a kind of meditation, a spiritual practice. For that matter, every task becomes a spiritual practice when we do it consciously with all our focus and devotion. The essence of a spiritual practice is that it lays emphasis on being present in the moment, paying close attention to what is happening in the moment, and growing in awareness with the moment.

The opposite of unitasking is multitasking. It is believed that a human mind can hold only a single thought at a time. Hence it is considered that unitasking is more productive than multitasking as multitasking reduces a person's productivity by creating mental conflicts and distractions between two or more tasks.

Power of Charity

"It is more blessed to give than to receive." (Acts 20:35).

Charity Believes in Giving and Receiving. Charity believes in both giving and receiving. Giving is more active form of positive energy than expressing a feeling of gratitude. Charity is absence of possessiveness and attachment. Charity is generosity, an absence of greed. Charity believes in giving for the needy and helping the poor (alms-giving). It is said that God lives among the poor.

As renowned Indian poet Rabindranath Tagore says in *Gitanjali*, his Nobel-prize winning book,

"Here is thy footstool and there rest thy feet where live the poorest, and the lowliest, and lost."

Charity is a form of service to the poor. Service to the poor through giving is the best form of worship. This is *karma yoga,* a noble life path to perfection.

As the Holy Hindu Scriptures, Dhammapada says,

> *"One should give even from a scanty store to him who asks."* (Dhammapada 224).

Giving always creates goodness in our lives; giving empowers and enriches our lives. *Giving is Receiving.* This value works in compliance with the universal law of cause and effect. The more we give the more we shall receive because giving creates sufficient space in our life for the abundant universal energy to be circulated freely and abundantly. This is the secret behind abundance and prosperity.

As the Holy Bible says,

> *"Give, and it will be given to you. Good measure, pressed down, shaken together, running over, will be put into your lap. For with the measure you use it will be measured back to you."* (Luke 6:37-38).

Charity Believes in Generosity

Charity is not mere giving; it is generous giving without withholding anything. Charity is cheerful giving. Cheerful, generous giving is the secret behind generous receiving.

As Saint Paul says,

> *"Now this I say, he who sows sparingly will also reap sparingly, and he who sows bountifully will also reap bountifully. Each one must do just as he has purposed in his heart, not grudgingly or under compulsion, for God loves a cheerful giver."* (2 Corinthians 9:6-7).

Generous giving fills us with a sense of pure joy, good will, and personal power. *"The generous will prosper; those who refresh others will themselves be refreshed."* (Proverbs 11:25). When we practice giving as a personal quality we realize that how rich we are. We all are inherently rich. We have a lot of things to give—our time and energy, knowledge, skills, talents, smile, kind words, appreciation, encouragement, motivation, inspiration, our listening ears, and finally, our money and wealth.

Charity is the Essence of Philanthropy

One of the top billionaires in the world, Bill Gates once stated in a press conference that his philanthropic gift worth USD 28 billion was motivated by his mother Mary who wrote to his wife Melinda Gates a wonderful biblical philosophy, which says,

"Much is required from the person to whom much is given; much more is required from the person to whom much more is given." (Luke 12:48)

Power of Gratitude

Giving believes in the power of charity while receiving believes in the power of gratitude. A humble heart is required to receive with an attitude of gratitude. The quality of being thankful is one of the superior human qualities. We should never hesitate to ask help from others in times of need but at the same time we need to be grateful for those help. We must receive from others with a grateful heart. Actually the word *'thank you'* should be an integral part of our daily communications. Charity begins at home but gratitude begins in a thankful heart. According to Cicero the legendary philosopher, gratitude is not only the greatest of virtues but the parent of all others. In former American President John Kennedy's words, *'we must find time to stop and thank the people who make a difference in our lives.'*

We all have a moral responsibility to be grateful for all our life's blessings. As Roman philosopher Seneca says,

"It is another's fault if he is ungrateful, but it is mine if I do not give. To find one thankful man, I will oblige a great many that are not so."

Gratitude is the Ability to Appreciate and Recognise Others' Efforts for Us. Every person on this planet craves for appreciation. Our mental health is directly related to how we are treated, appreciated and recognized by others.

Gratitude is the Ability to Appreciate Our Own Life and Count Our Blessings. We need to appreciate our life. We need to appreciate ourselves. The moment we appreciate ourselves we fall in love with ourselves. When we have love and appreciation for ourselves, we are in a position to love and appreciate others. In order to give away something to someone, first of all, we must possess that for ourselves.

We need to take a stock of all our blessings on a regular basis. And we must appreciate these blessings with a heart full of gratitude. When we recognize our blessings we become aware of the fact that how much blessed we are. When we recognize and appreciate a good thing in our life, its value is increased manifold as it is said that *Recognition Lubricates Energy Flow*.

It is quite easy for us to appreciate all the good things in our life. But we need to appreciate the bad things too. When we do that we respect the divine law of duality that is played out in our life. Hence we need to make it a habit to recognize and appreciate both good and bad things in our life. Remember, all bad things that happened in our life brought along with them a lot of valuable lessons. While we experienced the pain we were actually learning to have superior qualities such as strength and courage that were required to overcome that pain. In the process of tackling our life's bad experiences, we grew stronger and powerful. Nothing bad ever happens in a human life. Whatever happens is happening for a reason. So let's appreciate everything that comes along, no matter what it is, good or bad.

5 Laws of Appreciation and Gratitude

1. Always appreciate other people's presence in our life. Like them. They are God's gift to us.
2. Find a genuine reason to compliment them. Every person has a value in our life. Complimenting people actually boosts their morale and encourages them to do more good stuff for which they are being complimented.
3. Accept others the way they are. Never anticipate any change in the people who are in our lives. In order to change a person for the better, first of all, that person should be willing. Remember, everything begins with self.
4. Try to have an interesting and pleasant personality by remembering people's names and be friendly with them. Never bring an ego-based attitude in our relationships and social interactions. Nobody likes egotistical people.
5. Treat others fairly. Say 'please' and 'thank you' whenever necessary. Always listen to other's opinions with respect. Everyone has something to say. Listen to them with interest and appreciate their opinions genuinely.

CHAPTER 11

Personal Power System 2

"But let your "yes" be "yes" and your "no", "no"."(Matthew 5:37).

*P*ersonal Power System 2 comprises of Power of Truth, Compassion and Purity.

Power of Truth and Honesty

Truth is faith in the *Absolute Truth,* which is the Lord Almighty. Truth is a value which leads to truth speaking and truthful life. Truth speaking and truthful life are very simple to practice.

In Lebanese poet, Kahlil Gibran's words,

> *"Truth is a deep kindness that teaches us to be content in our everyday life and share with the people the same happiness."*

Honesty is the art of truth-speaking and straightforwardness. Honesty believes in truthful conduct. Without honesty, no one can travel the path of perfection.

As American Founding Father, Thomas Jefferson says,

> *"Honesty is the first chapter in the Book of Wisdom."*

Truth is Personal Integrity

Speaking truth is a virtue. Having honest confidence is a virtue. Honesty in all dealings is a virtue. Truth and honesty imparts integrity to one's personality. Integrity is the quality of being consistent in one's moral values, thoughts, speech and actions. Integrity is that quality of being honest and having strong moral principles. Integrity is having moral uprightness and forthrightness; having the courage to be straightforward in attitude and speech. A person of integrity is a reliable and trustworthy person. Therefore, the most desirable personality is a personality having integrity and honest confidence.

Truth is Transparency and Accountability

A truthful person is accountable for own life. When people become accountable for their own life, they break free of their negative and destructive thought pattern. 'Being accountable' means 'being true to oneself'. 'Being true to oneself' means 'being open to all experiences of life', both good and bad.

Truth Leads Us to Contemplation on Death

Human life is based on an eternal truth, i.e. while individual spirit is immortal, human body comes with an expiry date. Body expires and becomes useless on the date of expiry. Hence the only thing that we can do while we are alive is to live a full life based on truth and honesty. Indian poet Rabindranath Tagore portrayed death as a desirable guest in his Nobel-prize winning book 'Gitanjali'.
As he says,

"On the day when death will knock at thy door what will thou offer to him? Oh, I set before my guest the full vessel of my life—I will never let him go with empty hands."

Death is a truth. We all need to contemplate on this truth occasionally. It helps us overcome the hidden fear of death and we realize that death is not permanent it is just a passing phase. No one in the human world can avoid death. Death is a truth.
As Sri Gautama Buddha says,

"A place to live unharmed by death does not exist not in space, not in the sea, nor if you stay in the midst of mountains."

Power of Compassion

Compassion is the Virtue of Non-Injury and Non-Violence. Compassion is the ability of being merciful to everyone. Compassion is kindness, having a kind attitude towards everyone.

As American author Mark Twain says,

> *"Kindness is a language which the deaf can hear and the blind can see."*

Compassion is kind in speech and actions; it takes special care not to injure anyone with harsh speech, or harsh actions. Compassion is the fundamental value of all religions.

As His Holiness Dalai Lama, Spiritual Leader of Tibetan Buddhism says,

> *"This is my simple religion. There is no need for temples; no need for complicated philosophy. Our own brain, our own heart is our temple. The philosophy is kindness."*

Compassion is considerate to all human beings irrespective of caste, creed and race. Compassion is a person's ability to understand others as well as one self. When compassion grows in size the person is able to develop the gift of empathy. Empathy is the key ingredient of emotional intelligence.

Power of Purity

Definition of Purity

The value of purity is relevant to all three dimensions of our life, *body*, *mind* and *spirit*. Purity of body is called cleanness which is observed in clean and simple living.

As Rabindranath Tagore says in Gitanjali,

> *"Let me make my life simple and straight, like a flute of reed for thee to fill with music."*

In clean living focus is on perfect health. Perfect body (healthy body) leads to a perfect mind and a perfect mind leads to a perfect spirit. Body, mind and spirit are interconnected. If body is not perfect or unhealthy, mind and spirit suffers. If mind is not perfect, body and spirit suffers. That is, pure and perfect body leads to pure and perfect mind and spirit. Similarly, a pure mind leads to a pure body and spirit. People who are spirit-oriented believe in clean living as *cleanliness is next to godliness.*

Perfect Body—Health and Wellness

"Of all gains, good health is the greatest." (Dhammapada 203, the Hindu Scriptures).

We have a need to focus on right nutrition and regular physical exercise on a daily basis, for health is wealth. A balanced diet and regular exercise should form an integral part of our daily routine. *Sound mind resides in a sound body.* A healthy body has a sound physiology. A sound bodily physiology results in sound mind and right mental state. In a right mental state, one will have healthy thought process. Since our actions and behaviors have their origin in our thoughts, a sound mind leads to right behavior and a positive attitude towards life. In fact, keeping our body in good health is our primary duty.

As Sri Gautama Buddha says,

"To keep the body in good health is a duty, otherwise we shall not be able to keep our mind strong and clear."

Simplicity and Clean Living

Simplicity is the essence of a beautiful, clean and peaceful living. So simplify life. With growth comes sophistication and complexity. Since complexity alienates us from our unique nature, we need to take utmost care to preserve our simplicity. Being simple is being beautiful. Simplicity is attractive and easy to adopt as a life style.

The philosophy of a beautiful life lies in simplicity. It's so simple to live when it's so simple to love. It's so simple to win over many hearts when we know it's so simple to smile. Simplicity is the original sophistication.

As Leonard da Vinci, the great Italian painter says,

"Simplicity is the ultimate sophistication."

Perfect Mind and Spirit—
the Power of Human Mind and Spirit

General belief is that a human mind is the seat of consciousness (awareness), intelligence, emotions and feelings, memory and free will. However, the truth is that none of the neuroscientists, psychologists and philosophers in the world was able to define 'mind' and 'spirit' in a satisfactory manner till date. There are multitudes of psychological theories and philosophies pertaining to the mind and mind processes. However, we are still unable to get a vivid picture of our own mind and its activities and its relation with 'the Spirit'.

Mind as a Part of Human Brain

Modern-day neuroscientists believe that there is a strong correlation between human brain and mind because the mental capabilities of a person are considerably reduced in case of traumatic brain injuries and diseases like Alzheimer's syndrome.

Mind as an Independent Existence

According to Greek philosophers Plato and Aristotle, mind is independent of human body (brain). Vedanta philosophy also believes that mind is distinct from the physical body.

Mind Development

According to Vedanta philosophy, three-dimensional life (physical, intellectual and spiritual) is possible only through mind development. Mind can be a source of personal freedom or a field of bondage. How a person experiences 'duality of life' (sorrows and joys, strengths and weaknesses, faith and fear and so on) depends on the development and conditioning of the mind.

Power of human mind is unlimited; and we have power over our mind. We have unlimited mind power at our disposal. In order to tap into the vast potentialities of our mind, first of all, we need to understand the workings of our mind.

As Roman philosopher Marcus Aurelius says in his book 'Meditations',

> *"You have power over your mind, not outside events. Realize this, and you will find strength."*

It is believed that all our thoughts, memories, feelings and emotions originate in the realm of our mind. It is also believed that our mind is the seat of our free will. So in order to understand the workings of our mind we need to be aware of our thoughts, memories and emotions. We also need to be aware of conscious exercise of our free will.

Holistic Mind Development

A holistic mind development program takes care of thought management, emotion management, memory enhancement and development of will power.

Thought Management

The individual spirit is the animating principle or life force of a human body. This life force is always in a state of circulation (vibration) throughout the human body and outside the human body. All our thoughts, emotions, feelings and memories are made up of subtle energy vibrations. In a human body, thoughts are considered as one of the most intense form of energy vibrations. It is said that human thoughts can penetrate even 'time and space'. Yes, thoughts are that powerful.

Thoughts and destiny are interlinked. We are the products of our thoughts and our thoughts determine our destiny. Thoughts lead to speech; speech leads to actions and behaviors; actions and behaviors lead to habits, and habits form character, and finally, character determines destiny.

As Parsi Saint Zoroaster says,

"Taking the first step with a good thought, the second with a good word, and the third with a good deed, I entered paradise."

The beginning point to enter into a state of perfection is to be aware of our thoughts. Since thoughts are objects of the mind, thoughts must be regulated within the realm of mind itself. The beauty of a human mind is that it is capable of managing its own thought process. By regulating our thoughts in a desirable way we can create our own destiny. We are no more the children of fate if we know how to regulate our thoughts.

Law of Mind is Law of Visualization: Thoughts are present in our inner world. Our actions and behaviors are manifested in the outer world. Inner world determines outer world. *As within, so without.* This is the essence of the universal law of correspondence.

What is created in the mental plane will be manifested in the physical plane in the right time. This is the secret behind planning and visualization. We create a mental picture of what we want. Then, according to the universal law of action, we execute our plan through right efforts until desired results are achieved. i.e. Visualization directs realization of our goals.

Visualization is the art of imagination. There are two forms of imagination, synthetic imagination and creative imagination. Synthetic imagination is the result of education, experience and observation. Creative imagination is a gift, with which *'limited intelligence'* of a human being communicates with *the Infinite Intelligence*.

Managing Negativity through Sense Control

In a human being, the chain of thought process is mainly triggered through five sensory inputs—sight (eyes), smell (nose), touch (skin), taste (tongue) and hearing (ears). So by disciplining our senses, we can control undesirable thoughts up to some extent. Sense control can be achieved through firmness of will (will power).

Managing Negativity in Life

Negativity in our life can be managed through positive thinking. Positive thinking is thinking only positive thoughts filled with love, hope and optimism. Think only those thoughts that fill us with positive emotions like love, happiness, smile, joy, peace, and kindness. Positive thinking also allows us to replace our unpleasant thoughts with positive ones. Whenever, negative thoughts occur, we need to cancel it out with some good thoughts. Positive thinking is the secret behind a positive mental attitude.

As mystic poet Kahlil Gibran says,

"Your living is determined not so much by what life brings to you as by the attitude you bring to life; not so much by what happens to you as by the way your mind looks at what happens."

If our inner world is full of negative thought forces, we produce negative actions. Similarly, an inner world full of positive forces produces positive actions. Therefore the key to perfect mental health is positive thinking. Think positive thoughts and live a positive life. Regular practice of positive thinking fills a person with hope and optimism; and in no time, positive mental attitude becomes a part of that personality.

We need to be vigilant enough to avoid negative people, negative situations and unpleasant relationships in our life. Negative people are full of fears and doubts. They do not trust anyone, and they take their unhappiness and inferiority with them wherever they go. Sometimes we may end up absorbing their negative energy through their association. So it is always wise to avoid such people in our life.

We can attract positive energy into our life through positive living. Positive living is living a positive life by surrounding ourselves with positive people, good books, peace and serenity. We can preserve and conserve our inherent positive energy for a positive living. Never waste our precious energy in pleasing everybody because it is impossible to please everybody. Good people cannot please bad people and vice versa. Never waste our positive energy in justifying our actions after they are committed. Sometimes, a clarification may be necessary to avoid any misunderstandings. Then, by all means, do it. If possible live peaceably with all people by avoiding conflicts. For conflicts consume a lot of our precious energy, time and resources. It damages relationships.

Keeping a Journal for Thought Clarity

A human mind is continuously bombarded with multitudes of thoughts, both constructive and destructive. Keeping a journal to record all our constructive thoughts helps us organize our thoughts. We, then, become aware of our own thought pattern and the quality of our thoughts.

Low quality thoughts produce low quality actions. By all means, no one in the world would want a life of low quality actions. So keeping a journal allows us weed out all those poor quality thoughts, thus propelling us on the path of right thoughts and right actions. Thought clarity aided by journal writing helps us make right decisions. As lack of decision-making ability is the root cause of many of our worries and failures, keeping a journal is the best way to manage this scenario. Decision-making ability helps us to master the habit of procrastination.

Emotion Management

Emotion management is another aspect of developing mind power. Emotions are also objects of the mind and hence must be regulated within the mind. Most often, it so happens that thoughts may be controlled up to some extent, but our emotions often betray us. Almost always, our silly human emotions become more powerful and dominating in our minds than our logical thoughts. Still we do not complain. After all, the essence of a human life is the ability to experience different kinds of emotions. The beauty of a human life lies in its feelings and emotions. However, as progressive human beings we do not want to get stuck in the realm of feelings and emotions because emotional baggage and intellectual prejudices become the biggest hindrances for us to access the vast potential latent within our mind. Moreover, if we experience a negative emotion and do not find a vent to it, this suppressed negativity may leak into other realms of our life. Therefore we would like to manage our emotions in a successful manner for a perfect living.

Transient Nature of Emotions

Emotional needs are the most fundamental needs and emotional sufferings are the most painful experiences. Emotions are transient in nature. When we understand this transient nature of emotions, we overcome emotional conflicts. This state is, indeed, a major victory on the path to perfection. Reaching a mental state where we are free from all kinds of emotions is necessary to reach the point of perfection. Then we are no more 'humane', we are 'divine'. We have made the successful journey from 'being humane' to 'being divine', being just perfect.

The essence of 'being humane' is to 'have all kinds of human emotions'; to experience these emotions and to learn from them and to learn their effect on our psyche (spirit). There are binding emotions and liberating emotions. Binding emotions are centered on sensual pleasures and ego satisfaction. These emotions are obsessive, possessive and destructive. For example, lust is obsessive and binding. Hatred is destructive. Anger disturbs a human body's endocrine system (functioning of glands and associated hormones).

Liberating and Binding Emotions

Liberating emotions are liberating, creative and constructive. It frees a person from all bodily bondages, mental blocks and limitations. Liberating emotions are rooted in altruism. For example, love is liberating and creative. Forgiveness purifies heart and brings joy. When a person experiences liberating emotions like love, joy and forgiveness, it uplifts the lower self to merge with the higher self. And 'the Higher Self' is the field of immense potential and creativity. When a person experiences the binding emotions like lust, hatred and anger, it brings down the Higher Self to the Lower Self and thus corrupts it and in this field of 'Lower Self' inhabits the immense danger of the Evil. Binding emotions are destructive. These destructive emotions lead a person to destructive actions. Destructive emotions combined with destructive actions are the root cause of all human misery and sufferings.

Emotions and Relationships

Every person is a social animal. She/he wants to connect with people and wants to belong to a community. Living in a society means living with all kinds of emotions. Emotions may be good or bad. But the point is to know how to manage these emotions. Successful emotions management is an important step that we take towards 'creating the destiny' that we desire.

Human kind is meant to form relationships—loving and healthy relationships. There are different kinds of relationships, parent-child relationship, sibling relationships, husband-wife relationship, friendships, and so on. Different degrees of different emotions are felt in each of these relationships. All these relationships are meant for fulfilling our emotional needs, thus encouraging our progress on the path of perfection. The fundamental principles behind a successful relationship are love and trust. Relationships are meant for nurturing and growth. We do not have to categorize or name a relationship if the relationship is an association of two or more pure minds. Every relationship must be respected and nurtured as such on the basis of the purity of that relationship and the level of understanding between the individuals involved in that relationship. Some relationships do not have names and most often such 'nameless' relationships become the source of joy for an individual than any of blood-relationships.

Ups and downs are part of every relationship. Every 'down' stage in a relationship is a blessing in disguise for us as during this dark phase of life we practice the supreme qualities of patience (ability to wait for the right time to get things better), forgiveness (ability to let go), kindness (compassion), and pure love. By practicing the supreme qualities we get stronger mentally. Every relationship is meant to last forever. Every relationship provides an opportunity to grow together through learning together. Having that someone with us always makes us confident and self-assured. We experience all kinds of emotions in our companionships and relationships. Healthy relationships are the source of our personal security. We feel secure, happy and liberated in healthy and loving relationships.

Outward Expression of Negative Emotions

Every person wants to feel all kinds of positive emotions like love, joy, peace, pleasure, loyalty, companionship and friendship. None of us wants to have negative emotions like fear, hatred, resentment, pain and jealousy. Still we end up having more negative emotions than positive ones because it is human tendency to focus more on negativity than on positivity. Our natural tendency is to give a vent to all our negative emotions. But this behaviour is not desirable for social situations. That is, outward expression of negative emotions is an inappropriate behavior for social situations.

We need to control our undesirable manners and behavior patterns. We need to develop appropriate behavior patterns that are suitable for specific occasions. Always remember, the more we expose our vulnerabilities, the higher are the chances that others will control us.

However, in certain situations it is very important that we let the concerned people know how their behaviour affects us negatively through outward expressions. For example, it is better to give a vent to our anger than bottling it up within ourselves in such situations. Such 'bottling up' of negative emotions has dangerous consequences and often result in serious illnesses such as stroke, cancer and heart attack. So sometimes it is better to express all our negative emotions. This is recommended only if we are able to manage these emotions within our self-control. Experiencing a negative emotion makes us understand that how bad it is for our heart and brain. Our life is not to waste over petty negative emotions. Our life is too important to lose to small emotions like anger, hatred and jealousy. We are more precious than everything else. So we must always try to save ourselves from all negative emotions and mental conflicts. This is possible only through successful emotion management.

Developing Will Power and Power of Choice

"You have a choice between life and death; you will get whichever you choose." (Sirach 15:17).

Another important aspect of developing mind power is through the development of will power. Free will is the biggest gift of humanity. By exercising will power, we can control our thoughts, emotions, and actions. Will power is the secret behind our power of choice.

We are blessed with freedom of choices and we have to make right choices in order to enjoy the fruits of a successful life.

As Saint Paul says,

""All things are lawful for me," but not all things are helpful. "All things are lawful for me," but I will not be enslaved by anything." (1 Corinthians 6:12).

What we are today is the result of choices that we have made in the past and our future depends on the choices that we are making in every moment of our present life. Life is all about making right choices. In the Holy Bible, *the Book of Genesis* mentions an important truth about a human life. We are free to do anything and everything. But everything is not good for us. It is humane to crave for a variety of experiences. Most often we are not even sure about the nature of such experiences and its outcomes; whether it brings happiness and growth to us or it will simply destroy our God-given spirit. Here we have to use our judgment and common sense to make right choices. Another foundation on which we can make right decisions is our core value systems.

God never makes mistakes. If He wants us to use our free will to its full potential, He creates such circumstances in our life so that we grow in awareness of the gift of free will and its power of choices.

As the Holy Bible says,

"For you formed my inward parts; you knitted me together in my mother's womb. I praise you, for I am fearfully and wonderfully made. Wonderful are your works; my soul knows it very well. My frame was not hidden from you, when I was being made in secret, intricately woven in the depths of the earth. Your eyes saw my unformed substance; in your book were written, every one of them, the days that were formed for me, when as yet there was none of them." (Psalm 139:13-16)

Developing the 'power of will' is entirely in our hands and God desire us to develop this wonderful gift of humanity. Even though free will is a gift to the entire humanity, very few of us are able to develop it to its full potential. Because, great deeds require great sacrifices and very few people are ready to do great sacrifices.

According to the Scriptures, destiny plays an important role in our birth. Even the number of days in our life is pre-decided. We may not be able to change our birth circumstances (for example, we cannot change our parents and siblings, they are who they are) and enhance our life span, but one thing we can do. That is, the judicious use of the gift of freewill to create the destiny that we desire for ourselves. If we choose to follow the principles of Good and Right, we will reap the fruits of righteousness which is an abundant, prosperous, peaceful and happy life, a perfect life.

When we exercise discretion, rationality and sound judgment to make right choices, we develop a firmness of will. Strong will power is an important ingredient of a strong personality. When we have a strong personality with a firmness of will, we can control the negativity around us. We will, in no way, be affected by human beings or circumstances of lower nature. We will always depend upon our own decision-making ability to make choices. When we make right choices and right decisions, we can be the master of our own destiny.

One life time may not be sufficient to fulfil all the desires of the human body. However, one lifetime is sufficient to fulfil the desires of the Spirit. It is up to us to choose between the two. Decision is ours. Choice is ours. Power lies in the ability to make right choices. When we make right choices we become powerful; and personal power is the strongest forms of all powers.

Free will means we have freedom of choices. Since too many choices create confusion, we need to be aware of the sensible use of free will as freedom of free will implies responsibility; to be responsible for our own life. It is neither our pedigree or blue blood nor our education or circumstances which are responsible for our lives, it is us. We are responsible for our own lives, nobody else.

Since we have the freedom to choose, we are responsible for our choices. Sometimes there are too many choices that we do not know what to choose, how to choose. Here comes the significance of clarity of purpose. When we are clear about the purpose of our life, we do not have any confusion as to what to choose. Now we have made some choices that help us realize the purpose of our life. With choices come actions. With actions come results and consequences of those actions. If choices are right, results are also right. And we are on the path to perfection.

According to the Hindu Scriptures, *karma* (effect of our past and present actions on our life) may become a determining factor in a person's destiny only if the person allows it to be. With the power of free will, human beings are in a position to choose and to focus on those actions in their life which negate the evil effects of *karma*. Supreme qualities such as forgiveness and enlightenment (through the right study of the Holy Scriptures and good books) are the best answers to neutralize all the evil effects of *karma*.

Will Power and Self Mastery

Strong will power leads us to self control, a state of personal freedom where one is powerful enough to make right choices, *always*. Self control is the secret behind self mastery, the art of mastering oneself.

As legendary Chinese philosopher Lao Tzu says,

"Mastering others is strength. Mastering oneself makes one fearless."

Self mastery is a state of fearlessness and the ability to control oneself in a rightful manner. The supreme quality that leads a person to ultimate state of inner peace, happiness and perfection is self-mastery, the state of inner freedom. Self mastery relies on the belief that there is no limit for human potential, and therefore there is no limit for growth.

As Dhammapada, the Hindu Scriptures says,

"Freedom is ultimate happiness." (Dhammapada 205)

Personal freedom that is rooted in self mastery believes that every person has the freedom to make own life decisions; and the freedom to think good, to speak good and to do good.

As the mystic poet Kahlil Gibran says,

"Life without freedom is like a body without a soul, and freedom without thought is like a confused spirit."

Let us free ourselves from the bondages of body and mind. Let us refuse to be a victim of self-pity and others' sympathy. We all have vast free space and tremendous freedom within. What we have to do is just go back to the space within and feel free to move around. Atharva Veda, one of the four Vedas of the Hindu Scriptures extols the virtue of personal freedom.

As Atharva Veda says,

"Open yourself; create free space; release the bound one from his bonds. Like a new born child freed from the womb, be free to move on every path."

Personal Freedom Should Be Used Judiciously: We should never play psychological games to win our selfish objectives or to influence others. A truly great person does not require psychological manipulations and deceptions to enhance her/his greatness. There is no one more powerful in the world than a person of integrity, character, and intelligence. Psychological manipulations within trusted relationships are taken for granted by many of us.

We all have weaknesses; and our major weaknesses are our own loved ones—people who love us and whom we love. But it is also true that we expect a lot from our loved ones. Parents expect their children to behave in a certain way, and children expect their parents to do more for them. To reach these goals, we immediately resort to trivial emotional manipulations and mind games, sometimes knowingly, and most of the times unknowingly, to influence the decision-making process of our near and dear ones. We use brainwashing to influence them to think in a certain way. We use different mind tricks for emotional blackmailing of our own people. However, such practices, in the long term, result in mistrust and loss of love as true love is selfless. True love helps others grow strong physically, mentally and spiritually. True love lets others be what they are.

Personal Freedom is a State of Independence: Personal freedom moves from dependence to independence to interdependence. As an evolving person, each one of us wants to grow towards independence and later to interdependence.

First stage of this journey is to be free from all kinds of dependence. When we're dependent on others, financially, emotionally, physically, mentally, intellectually, and spiritually, then we become aware of the limitations of being dependent. These limitations actually imprison a person in own fears and insecurities and the person always craves to break free of 'dependence' habit. Dependence is a habit meant for the parasites and the blood-sucking leeches. Dependence will never be able to be in a position to provide.

After overcoming dependence habit, the person has to develop self reliance in everything. Self help is the best help and God helps only those who help themselves. The best way to develop this self-reliance or habit of independence is to train on life skills such as self confidence, self esteem, self respect and self control. Only a person, who has grown out of the dependence habit can grow to the level of independence.

Similarly, only a person who has grown to the level of independence can further grow to the level of interdependence. Interdependence is the ability of a person to form healthy networking with similar-minded people. The secret of a healthy interdependence state is the collective spirit of the group. Interdependence is the secret behind successful teamwork.

When a person is able to reach the stage of interdependence, that person reaches the state of 'Providence" where the person assumes the position of the Giver.

5 Laws of Emotion Management

1. Understand the transient nature of emotions
2. Understand the effects of liberating and binding emotions on human psyche
3. Replace binding emotions with liberating emotions to have the feeling of liberation and personal freedom
4. Form healthy relationships that help us grow and evolve
5. Control outward expression of negative emotions through self control

CHAPTER 12

Personal Power System 3

"A good person brings good out of the treasures of good things in his heart."
(Luke 6:45)

*P*ersonal *Power System 3 Comprises of Power of Goodness. Goodness is Radiance of Character.*

Power of Goodness and Good Deeds

"Doing good to others is not a duty. It is a joy, for it increases your own health and happiness."—Zoroaster, Founder of Zoroastrianism

Goodness is moral excellence, the excellence in practicing all virtues. Power of goodness is power of virtues. Goodness is the inner radiance of a person that reflects a strong character.

As Yajur Veda, the Hindu Scriptures says,

"Attractiveness and magnetism of your personality is the result of your inner radiance."

Good deeds are the most honourable things both in the sight of God and the human beings. Our goodness is our 'divine protection'. Goodness in us can conquer the evil in others.

We all are influenced by the goodness of other people. Goodness in a woman and/or in a man is the most attractive quality that inspires and motivates us. Their goodness attracts us like a magnet towards them. We look up to them as our role models. We admire them for their good qualities. Sometimes we are so much influenced by them that we try to imitate their actions just to discover to our dismay that we are totally incapable of doing what they do. We soon realize that it requires an earnest desire, the strength of will power, conscious effort and constant practice to cultivate the goodness within us. It requires a lot of sacrifices to become a good person and to do the good deeds. Yes, goodness is reserved for those who have strength of character. Goodness is not a weakness rather it is a mighty power.

Our goodness is not a license for others to take advantage of us. We should never allow weak people to take an upper hand on us at the cost of our good nature. What we need to do is to understand human nature and modify our behaviour according to the gravity of the situation and the nature of the people whom we deal with. Sometimes acting harshly may become an inevitable behaviour choice in certain unavoidable circumstances for getting desirable (positive) results. After all, what matters most is the result of an action and the pure motive behind every action. If motive is good, all actions that are in compliance with our core values are justified.

Goodness is a choice; it is in everyone's capacity to make a choice of being compassionate for those who struggle to meet their survival needs—food, water, shelter and clothes.

As the Holy Bible says,

"For I was hungry and you gave me food, I was thirsty and you gave me drink, I was a stranger and you welcomed me, I was naked and you clothed me, I was sick and you visited me, I was in prison and you came to me." (Matthew 25:35-36).

Goodness is a habit. Goodness comes from a constructive mind. The seeds of this habit are sown in our minds the moment we make a covenant with ourselves to be a good person and to do the good deeds. Let us take the resolution of *'being a better person'* on a fine morning of a fine New Year day. From that day onwards, let us make it a practice to think good thoughts, to speak kind words, and to do the good deeds. Life is all about making right choices. Our choices are reflected in our actions. Our actions bear a witness to our speech.

As Saint James says,

"You see that a person is justified by works and not by faith alone." (James 2:24)

CHAPTER 13

Personal Power System 4

There is no fear in love; but perfect love casteth out fear; because fear hath torment. He that feareth, is not made perfect in love. (John 4:18)

Personal Power System 4 Comprises of Power of Love and Forgiveness.

Definition of Love

Love is the highest form of energy vibration within us; the most potent force in the universe. Highly extolled value of a human being is the ability to love and to be loved. Love is fearless. Love is absence of wrath, hatred and anger. All of us, irrespective of their country of origin, caste, religion, social status, financial status, education and career, have the ability for '*being open to love*' and for '*being in love*'. We all have the power to love. We can love anyone without any conditions.

There are three types of love, *eros* (romantic love); *philos* (brotherly love) and *agape* (unconditional love). *Eros* is romantic love which is essential for a perfect marriage. *Eros* is passionate and intense. *Eros* is expressed in passionate feelings and blind emotions. *Philos* is brotherly or sisterly love which is expressed in other intimate relationships such as friendships and love for siblings. *Agape* is unconditional love; it is the ability to love unconditionally without expecting anything in return. *Agape* just loves. *Agape* just accepts everything. Agape is genuine, strong and pure. Among three types of love, *agape* is the highest form of love. In order to experience 'agape', we must be ready to renounce all expectations from our relationships. Expectations taint the purity of love, therefore the purity of the relationship.

We all are capable of unconditional love, a love that is pure and devoid of even subtle manipulation and deception. For most of us just the feeling of 'being in love' is sufficient to energize and revitalize our whole human existence. The feeling of love provides us with a new vitality, and a new purpose of life. In the process of 'being in love' and 'be loved', we become refined and progress into better human beings. The most fundamental emotional need of a person is love. Outward expression of love accelerates the development of spiritual intelligence inherent in all of us.

There is love for God, love for oneself, love for parents, love for family and friends, love for the society and in a broader term, love for the world and the environment. The beauty of human life is that one can experience all these different dimensions of love in a single life time. And when we experience love, we experience God.

As the Holy Bible says,

> "*No one has ever seen God, but if we love one another, God lives in union with us, and his love is made perfect in us.*" (1 John 5:11).

Love is Forgiveness

Love is forgiveness. *Forgiveness is letting go of negativity while keeping our inherent supreme energy uncorrupted.* There is power in love and forgiveness. According to M K Gandhi, India's national father, "*The weak can never forgive. Forgiveness is the attribute of the strong.*"

When we forgive others' atrocities, we love them and most importantly, we love ourselves. In non-forgiveness we harbor emotions like anger and resentment. These emotions are negative forces and self destructive. These negative emotions are incompatible with the positive forces of our individual spirit.

It is discussed before that it is *impossible* for the human spirit to hold both negative and positive forces at the same time. One or other must dominate. That is, it is impossible for a human being to feel peaceful and agitated at the same time. Either the person has to be peaceful or agitated; not both at the same time. Love and forgiveness are the strongest forces that cleanse the Spirit of the negative forces and make it clean so that it can hold '*agape*', the strongest of all spiritual forces.

We can give pure and accepting love only from a pure and accepting heart. If we want to send out pure love from us, first of all, we must possess it. We can take out only from the treasures that we hold. If we do not have it, we cannot give it. If we hold the treasure of love and forgiveness within us, we have the power to set ourselves free from the bonds of negative emotions. By seizing that power, we can rise above the pains and negativities of the life. We can rise to the level of perfection.

Almost all relationships are based on expectations. When expectations are not met, we are hurt. We get disappointed in those relationships. We want to run away from those relationships in order to avoid further emotional wounds. When we carry all these emotional wounds without forgiving those who have caused them, then we live our lives like 'walking corpses'. The beauty of forgiveness is that it helps us make alive again and gives us immense strength to bear all kinds of emotional wounds. If love is to be experienced, then emotional wounds are inevitable. What we need is the strength to bear our emotional wounds lightly and with a good will. True love is reserved only for those who have the strength to forgive; and the strength to bear all emotional wounds with an attitude of goodwill and peace.

Love is Absence of Indifference

In modern times, apathy or indifference, most often, becomes a necessary mechanism of self-preservation. However, indifference is a sin; it is a non-virtuous action. We all have a moral obligation to be responsible for the welfare of the other people and the society. The strength of the evil lies in indifference of good people. The evil can successfully instigate evil people to form evil groups where good people become mere onlookers. *The Evil* can use the power of unity to oppress the causes that good people are fighting for. Sometimes the good people are too forgiving and too patient that they let the evil to gain strength more and more at the cost of their indifference and inaction.

Love Believes in Justice for All

Justice is a moral principle which is characteristic of an evolved person. Justice believes in treating everyone fairly. Fairness is a virtue that is free from all prejudices and biases. Fairness is being fair-minded in all our actions, and treating everyone with fairness and respect. Fairness calls for an unbiased approach to all situations and people. It inculcates decency and correctness in one's behaviour and thus ensures justice in all dealings.

In other words, justice believes in equality and fair play. Justice is a quality that is shown by those who are upright in their heart and righteous in their behaviour. Justice is moral uprightness based on ethics and values. We need to respect all those people who have a sense of justice and fairness.

In fairness and justice, we develop a sense of dignity. We realize that it is our fundamental right to protect our dignity as well as that of others. If one of us is abused or being wronged, we make sure that we get the situation right. And we never allow powerful people to manipulate weaker sessions of the society. Whenever we witness the exploitation and maltreatment of weaker sessions of the society, it is our duty to stand for them and speak for their rights. At the same time we need to be aware of our limitations. It is literally impossible for us to go beyond our limitations to change the societal behaviors as a whole. What is in everyone's capacity is to empower the weak and the poor through various means such as providing employment and education.

The reality of life is that every person has a destiny. All have their respective burdens to carry. We are not responsible for the destiny of our fellow beings. However, we may be able to help them find the right path. We may be able to empower the weak. But ultimately their destiny is their own creation. No one else is responsible for it. Similarly, we cannot hold anyone else or external circumstances responsible for our life and destiny. We create our destiny with our own actions.

Love is Non-judgment and Acceptance

One of the favorite biblical quotes of American president Abraham Lincoln was, "*Judge not, that you be not judged*". In fact, most of the people with whom we interact in our daily life are not worried for themselves or for their self development. They are worried about others. They do not have any time left for themselves after criticizing others and poking their noses in other people's affairs. They are much more worried about other's growth and development rather than their own growth and development.

In our life situations also these people are always ready to point out our deficiencies and mistakes, most often unasked, and give us a lot of unwanted advices as if we do not know anything about our own life. Such hypocrisy is to be ridiculed.

As the Holy Bible says,

"You hypocrite, first take the log out of your own eye, and then you will see clearly to take the speck out of your brother's eye." (Matthew 7:5).

The truth is that we all love to be corrected and directed on the right path. But we need to make sure that whether the people who are ready to guide us are qualified, eligible and capable to do so; whether they understand us well; whether they have our welfare and growth in their mind as the top priority.

Non judgment is Acceptance of Everything and Everyone

Non-judgment is absence of hypocrisy, criticism and indifference. Non-judgment is absence of fault-finding. Non-judgment stays away from slandering or calumny. A person having non-judgment attitude respects and accepts everyone. i.e. Non-judgement is acceptance and tolerance for everyone and everything.

Acceptance is an emotional state of a person who accepts and understands the reality of a situation, without attempting to change it. The art of acceptance is the art of tolerance. Acceptance is our capacity to tolerate whatever life brings us, whether good or bad. Acceptance and tolerance may also refer to the capability of a person to respect the beliefs of others. When we have acceptance and tolerance, we accept others the way they are.

Acceptance is a positive attitude that says '*I am OK. You are OK*'. It is a positive attitude which knows that God alone is perfect and we all are human beings with all human weaknesses.

As the Holy Bible says,

"None is righteous, no, not one; no one understands; no one seeks for God. All have turned aside; together they have become worthless; no one does good, not even one." (Romans 3:10-18).

Acceptance is surrender, complete surrendering to God's' will. It eliminates all anxieties from mind. Our journey is towards perfection. The moment we focus on our own perfection, addressing all the weaknesses within us in a systematic and positive manner, without fearing to acknowledge them, we begin to walk on the path of perfection.

When we are perfect we have every right to focus on others' imperfections and then we can take the courage to correct them. Now the big question is, *Am I perfect now*? This is the question each of us should ask to ourselves. In the Holy Bible there is a story of a woman who was caught in adultery by a group of people and was brought before Jesus Christ for judgment. Jesus asks them, *"Who among you are sinless? Let them judge her."* So the journey towards perfection is definitely not an easy one. The point of perfection where we can *'be all that we can be'* is not in our immediate grasp. It requires conscious effort, practice, and regular focus on perfecting ourselves in all aspects of our life.

CHAPTER 14

Personal Power System 5

"Gentleness, self-control; against such things there is no law."
(Galatians 5:23)

Personal Power System 5 Comprises of Power of Self Control. Self Control is the Art of Self Mastery

Definition of Self Control

Self-control is the highest form of self regulation. This is the art of self mastery. We all may be able to control our speech, behaviors, habits and actions up to some extent. However, persons of high degree of self control are able to regulate even their thoughts, emotions and feelings. Such persons are in full control of their life. They are the masters of their own destiny because there is no law which is higher than self control.

Self Control through Sense Control

Sense control is an integral part of self control. Actually self control begins when we practice controlling or regulating our five senses—eyes, ears, nose, skin, and tongue. Self control is within our call when we practice sense control.

In fact, a human life is meant to experience different kinds of worldly pleasures. We experience these worldly pleasures mainly through our senses. That is, our sensory pleasures become our major worldly experiences. But the irony of life is that once a human life is trapped in the realm of sensory pleasures alone, that life becomes incapable of experiencing higher pleasures such as intellectual, aesthetic and moral pleasures. Perfection of a human life happens only when a person is able to move beyond the realm of sensory pleasures to the realm of higher subtle pleasures such as intellectual, aesthetic and moral pleasures. Gradually, the person is able to move from the realm of these subtle pleasures to highest form of pleasure, i.e. perfection.

Lower Pleasures vs. Higher Pleasures

Pleasure is absence of pain. It is deeply rooted in human nature to desire a pain-free life and to indulge in all pleasurable experiences. There is a sect of people who believe that 'pleasure' is the ultimate end of a human life. Therefore they struggle against all natural difficulties to attain a 'pleasurable life', which is devoid of pains and discomforts. There are mainly four types of pleasures—sensory (bodily) pleasures, intellectual pleasures, aesthetic pleasures and moral (mental) pleasures.

Renowned English philosopher John Stuart Mill defines two kinds of pleasures in his book '*Utilitarianism*'—Lower Pleasures and Higher Pleasures. According to him, sensory pleasures are lower pleasures, and higher pleasures include intellectual pleasures (acts involving intellectual complexity), aesthetic pleasures (acts engaging the aesthetic imagination) and moral pleasures (acts involving moral sentiments).

For some of us the goal of life may be pursuit of all kinds of sensory pleasures. But the Holy Scriptures emphasizes on the truth that "*Kingdom of God is not food and drink.*" (Romans 14:17) Pursuit of sensory pleasures as a goal of life is actually antagonistic with the noblest goal of a human life i.e. personal perfection.

Sensory pleasures are those pleasures derived out of the immediate gratification of sense desires. Sight, smell, touch, taste and hearing are major sensory functions and a specific pleasure experience is associated with each of these sensory perceptions. Some of the examples are, tasting wine or coffee, listening to music, and eating a good dinner. Too much focus on sensory pleasures actually degrades a human spirit.

As the Holy Bible says,

"*Now the works of the flesh are evident: sexual immorality, impurity, sensuality, idolatry, sorcery, enmity, strife, jealousy, fits of anger, rivalries, dissensions, divisions, envy, drunkenness, orgies, and things like these. I warn you, as I warned you before, that those who do such things will not inherit the kingdom of God.* (Galatians 5:19-21)

John Stuart Mill equates sensory pleasures to 'animal appetites'. According to him a human life rich in lower pleasures is not a happy human life at all as human beings have faculties more elevated than the animal appetites.

According to Mill's philosophy on pleasure, knowingly or unknowingly, most of the people prefer lower pleasures. Lower pleasures are the products of immediate gratification of bodily urges resulting in an intense pleasurable feeling. However such pleasures are short-lived and are often followed by a feeling of displeasure. Gratification of lower pleasures never leads to other pleasures. People caught up in the enjoyment of sensory pleasures will never evolve or grow. This eternal truth is explained beautifully by Jesus Christ in the Parable of the Sower.

"And as for what fell among the thorns, they are those who hear, but as they go on their way they are choked by the cares and riches and pleasures of life, and their fruit does not mature." (Luke 8:14)

Intellectual, Aesthetic and Moral Pleasures

Intellectual pleasures are derived out of the uses of intellectual functions of a human brain such as memorizing, analyzing, reasoning and thinking. For example, reading a book, playing chess, composing a music, and writing a book

Aesthetic pleasures are derived out of the uses of higher intellectual functions such as imagination and artistic expression of an idea. For example, admiring a painting, attending a musical concert, creating a landscape, or sculpting a sculpture

Moral pleasures are derived out of the uses of mental functions such as sentiments and application of moral values. For example, helping the poor people, or any kind of philanthropic work

In Mill's opinion, pleasures of the intellect, pleasures of the feelings and imagination, and pleasures of the moral sentiments are far superior and more valuable than lower pleasures. His major view points on pleasure and human life are,

1. Humans are not meant for the gratification of bodily pleasures
2. A sensual pleasure such as having physical intimacy with one's spouse may be more intense than an intellectual pleasure of reading a book. But the latter is far superior than the former
3. There are some greatest pleasures which are worthy enough to be pursued by a human being as noble ends as humans are meant for higher forms of life and capable of achieving it
4. 'Sense of Dignity', a feeling of self-worth is the utmost importance of a human life and that's what makes us what we are
5. People who lack the 'sense of dignity' may thoroughly enjoy living the life of a swine (animal) for dignity is not a part of their make up
6. Human beings have a task to fulfil, and that task is not the maximization of pleasure, instead they must bring themselves *'nearer to the ideal perfection of human nature'*

Why Are We Incapable Of Enjoying Higher Pleasures?

Pursuit of higher pleasures is not in everyone's capacity. Those who pursue higher pleasures are called intellectuals, artists, spiritualists and so on. An average human being is incapable of enjoying or pursuing higher pleasures because of a variety of factors.

John Stuart Mill summarises these factors as,

"Capacity for the nobler feelings is in most natures a very tender plant, easily killed, not only by hostile influences, but by mere want of sustenance; and in the majority of young persons, it speedily dies away if the occupations to which their position in life has devoted them, and the society into which it has thrown them, are not favourable to keeping that higher capacity in exercise."

Every person is a storehouse of tremendous potential. Every person is called to exercise the power of inherent higher capacity, the capacity of the higher mind. However, majority of people are unaware of this fact as their minds are fully occupied with their current life circumstances.

The truth is we all have an inherent power to rise above these limitations of life. And the power that makes us capable to do so is 'the power of self control', the art of self mastery. This is the power by which one can regulate or change one's life circumstances and individual limitations.

Self Awareness, the Beginning Point of Self Control

The beginning point of self control is self discipline, disciplining one's body and mind. Bodily discipline leads to mental discipline as body and mind are connected. When we discipline our body, we become aware of our thoughts which originate in the realm of our mental plane. The ability of being aware of one's own thoughts and actions is known as 'self awareness'. Self-awareness is to know what is happening now and to live in the present. Our inner world of thoughts determines our actions and behaviors in the outer world. So *'being self-aware'* means that being aware of both the inner and the outer world.

Self awareness begins with oneself and it is a state of being aware of one's own thoughts, emotions and feelings. It is actually a state of consciousness of what is being going on inside one's brain. Being aware of our own thoughts means that keeping a constant watch over our thought process. Management experts use the term *'metacognition'* for this human ability of knowing about one's own thought process. Initially it is very difficult for a human being to be aware of all those thoughts that are bombarding in his/her brain. There are multitudes of them and some are creative inspirations while others are destructive thoughts. Negative thought patterns induce depression while creative and happy thoughts enhance our mood. When we are aware of our own thoughts, we get insights into the effects of our thoughts on our psyche and therefore the need to manage our thought process in a healthy manner. Metacognition results in awareness of thinking process which in turn results in self awareness process.

There are two states of awareness: affirmative (positive) and negative. A positive person (spirit-oriented) will always be in an affirmative state of awareness because that person's thoughts are filled with positive forces. A negative person (ego-centered) will always be in a state of negative awareness about evil, poverty, hatred, resentment, greed and worry. A wise person will deliberately keep his/her consciousness in a state of affirmative awareness because affirmative awareness brings affirmative actions.

Self Awareness Leads to Mental Alertness

Self-awareness creates mental alertness. Mental alertness is very much needed to live in 'eternal now'. Only a mentally alert person can experience the joy of mindful living. Only an alert mind is capable to exercise full power of self control. Such a person is adept at channeling all life force into the higher force centers in order to pursue higher and nobler life purposes. An alert mind lives in the present moment. This is the art of living in present.

Living in present means that single-minded focus on the task at hand which is the secret behind creativity and productivity. When we live in present we automatically give up resistance to all unfavorable thoughts and actions because our focus is on the present moment. We forget about past, focus on present and think about future. Living in moment or mindful living is living with full awareness of present moment, leaving the past behind and planning for a bright future.

As Saint Paul says,

"But this one thing I do, forgetting those things which are behind, and reaching forth unto those things which are before, I press toward the mark for the prize of the high calling of God in Christ Jesus." (Philippians 3:13-14).

When we are living in a state of mental alertness, we become intuitively aware of the boundaries that are to be kept in our relationships with other people; we become aware of our strengths and weaknesses. We will become naturally aware of how to use the strengths and how to handle the weaknesses.

Not all human beings are blessed with the power of self-awareness and mental alertness. Human beings are born with different degrees of intelligence. Only an inherently intelligent person has the ability to analyze 'Self' and 'Life'. Only such a person becomes 'self-aware' in the process of multiple self-analyses and self-improvement activities. A person who is not aware of how she/he acts or feels in the physical and mental realms of existence will never progress on the path of perfection. However, if some external guidance is available to such persons from an enlightened master, or an enlightened spouse, or enlightened friends then they are also able to make progress in life. A self-aware person strives for a perfect living. Such persons are always eager for constant self-improvement and self-renewal activities. For such persons, life is not about *getting more* but *'being more'*.

If we are not aware of the workings of our own body and mind, we are not able to discipline ourselves. Self discipline is an ongoing life process. We begin with comparatively easy body disciplinary practices such as moderation in food consumption, and then later fasting and prayer, observing silence, and practicing religious rituals, in order to progress to the harder realm of mental discipline where we learn to discipline even our mind. Mental discipline is achieved through austere practices such as meditation, self-denial practices, and study of the Holy Scriptures. At the highest degree of mental discipline, our mind is trained to think only the thoughts that we want to think. A trained mind is the powerhouse of *supreme energy*; a disciplined mind is the storehouse of will power. Self control is the result of strong will power, the secret behind our mental power; our power to choose the right over the wrong. Self control helps us to resist temptations, instinctive impulses and undesirable behaviors in all life situations.

As the Holy Bible says,

"For God gave us a spirit not of fear but of power and love and self-control."(2 Timothy 1:7).

It is quite natural for human beings to respond to their natural urges and impulses. But all our urges and desires are not good for us.

As the Book of Sirach says,

"If you allow yourself to satisfy your every desire you'll be a joke to your enemies." (Sirach 18:31).

Persons who lack self control are impulsive, always yielding to their impulses and therefore repulsive. They give vent to all their impulses, urges, emotions and behaviors, no matter where they are, and who they are. A person who lacks self control is considered as an indecent person, a person who lacks sense of civility.

As the Book of Proverbs says,

"A man without self-control is like a city broken into and left without walls."(Proverbs 25:28).

Self control is a natural behaviour choice for a self-disciplined man in all undesirable circumstances.

As Sama Veda, one of the four Vedas of the Sacred Hindu Scriptures says,

"A man of restraint attains unfathomable powers by means of preservation and conservation of energy. He does not waste his energy in seeking sensual pleasures."

Benjamin Franklin, one of the Founding Fathers of the United States of America advised parents to train their children in the virtue of self control. He believed that a society that upholds self control as its fundamental value would be a crime-free society. As he says,

"Educate your children to self-control, to the habit of holding passion and prejudice and evil tendencies subject to an upright and reasoning will, and you have done much to abolish misery from their future and crimes from society."

Self Analysis, a Path to Self Discovery

Self-discipline leads us to self reflection. When we form the habit of self reflection—reflecting on our own thoughts, words and actions on daily basis—we automatically develop the habit of self analysis. Self-analysis is nothing but the realistic estimation of one's self worth. Such regular personal reflection sessions and associated self analyses accompanied by corrective measures taken by us to improve the areas where we are lacking, lead us to self-development. Self analysis guides a person to explore those areas of his/her life where self control is lacking. Backed by self analysis, a person can put in conscious effort to develop self control over those life areas where attention is required.

How to Do a Successful Self-Analysis Session?

1. Choose a peaceful quiet space
2. Sit in a relaxed position
3. Relax body and put mind in a reflective/meditative mood

4. Analyze the strengths (positive forces) and weaknesses (negative forces) of the Self
5. Note down both positive and negative behaviors on a journal
6. Acknowledge negative forces (negative energies or negative behaviors) of the Self. You cannot change what you do not acknowledge.
7. Decide to change these negative behaviors into a more acceptable behavior.
8. Focus on the negative behaviors one by one and determine to change them
9. Plan a time frame to make the changes happen
10. Get real and sincere with self-analysis by taking as much time as the process requires
11. Keep a regular tab on the improvement of the Self

Self Control is the Source of Self-Sufficiency

Self development on a regular basis, over a period of time, leads to self-sufficiency. A self-sufficient person is not influenced or controlled by others in matters of opinion and conduct. A self-sufficient person is an independent thinker. A self-sufficient person believes in self-help. The law of self-help states that *'God helps those who help themselves'*.

There is nothing free in this world. There is a price for everything; big or small, we will have to pay the price to gain something. And that price is self-effort. Remember, *no pain no gain*. We cannot change the world and the people around us in a single day. Eventually and gradually we may be able to make little differences. But now what we can do is to focus on ourselves and train ourselves to become independent and self-sufficient to fight the battle of life successfully.

The mindset of *'being independent'* gives an individual immense creative freedom and that person produces fruits that are unique and of high quality. A person who is independent is also confident and holds self in high esteem. Such a person has great self respect and treats others also with respect. And in the process that person is respected by all.

Self Control is the Source of Self-Confidence

Self-sufficiency leads to self respect and self-confidence. Confidence is a strong personal force. A self-confident person has a strong positive self-image and presents a strong projected image to the external world with a natural personality. A self-confident person has a strong self-belief and a high sense of self worth.

5 Laws of Self Confidence

1. Persons having self respect are respected by others and they have high self confidence
2. Persons who are highly competent in all areas of life will have higher self-confidence
3. Confident persons always rely on the inner competence, that they have acquired through a variety of life's experiences, in challenging life situations
4. Confident persons are also responsible and accountable for their life
5. Confident persons stand for what they believe in

CHAPTER 15

Personal Power System 6

"Develop a mind of equilibrium. You will always be getting praise and blame, but do not let either affect poise of mind; follow calmness, the absence of pride."
Sri Buddha

P*ersonal Power System 6 Comprises of Power of Inner Peace and Intuition.*

Definition of Inner Peace

Peace is a state of quietness, serenity and tranquility. Peace originates from a calm mind center, from a mind of equilibrium. Peace is an inner state of stillness, a state which is free from worries, fears and anxieties. Nothing can trouble a peaceful mind.

As the Book of Jobs says,

"When He giveth quietness, who then can make trouble?" (Job 2:10).

Inner peace begins the moment we choose not to allow another person or event to control our emotions. Peace begins with the understanding of our own inner world. For achieving inner peace, it has to be consciously cultivated through a set of practices. These are meditation and prayer, silence and solitude, chanting sacred words (*mantras*), spending time with nature, practicing religion and religious rituals, and through adequate rest and relaxation of body and mind. Inner peace may also be obtained through the association of good company and through practices such as detachment and renunciation.

Inner Peace through Meditation

Meditation is an act of contemplation. It is a technique by which one pays attention to the deeper levels of one's mind. In meditation, we let go of ordinary mental activities of thinking, analyzing, problem-solving and memorizing; instead we focus on higher mind and inner awareness. In meditation we focus on the *inherent peace* that lies within us. Meditation brings the peace within towards the surface.

As Christian Saint Augustine prays for this inherent peace,

"Lord, thou madest us for thyself, and we can find no rest till we find rest in thee."

How to Do a Simple Meditation?

Five important criteria for a successful meditation session are a peaceful meditation environment, a comfortable sitting position, stillness of the body, deep breathing and quietness of the mind.

1. Peaceful meditation environment: Choose a peaceful, quiet space
2. Comfortable sitting position
    a. Sit on the floor in a simple cross-legged position. Care should be given that the spine is aligned straight with the body while sitting
    b. If sitting on the floor is difficult, the practitioner may sit on a cushion or a thick folded blanket for more comfortable sitting. Placing a cushion or thick padding under buttocks will also help in the correct alignment of the spine
    c. If sitting cross-legged is difficult, the practitioner may sit comfortably in any of the relaxed sitting positions. However, simple cross-legged position is better
    d. Never sit in a curved position
3. Stillness of the body
    a. Keep the head, neck and trunk of the body aligned straight
    b. Close the eyes and the mouth
    c. Let all facial muscles relax
    d. Relax shoulders and arms
    e. Allow arms and palms rest on the knees

4. Deep serene breathing process
   a. Become aware of your breathing process—inhaling (IN) and exhaling (OUT)
   b. Notice whether the breathing process is shallow or deep (if you are doing shallow breathing that means you are not yet ready for correct breathing meditation. So you have to correct it through conscious efforts of deep breathing. Practicing deep breathing regularly makes your breathing process healthy.)
   c. Do deep breathing (abdominal breathing i.e. breathing diaphragmatically) in a rhythmic manner and count 'in' and 'out' several times until the mind becomes quiet. Breath awareness quiets the mind.
5. Quietness of the mind
   a. Allow the mind to become quiet and focused
   b. Focus on 'awareness within' for 15 minutes during initial periods of meditation. Meditation duration may be extended to 30 minutes to 1 hour depending on the progress of the practitioner on the path of meditation

Other points to remember

✓ Practice meditation with the same sitting position and in the same environment for better results
✓ It is not recommended to meditate while lying down as lying posture is not suitable for inducing mental alertness

Inner Peace through Prayer

A beautiful prayer can be found in the book of *Gitanjali*, the Nobel-prize winning book of Indian poet Rabindranath Tagore. It goes like this,

> This is my prayer to thee, my lord—strike, strike at the root of penury in my heart.
> Give me the strength lightly to bear my joys and sorrows.
> Give me the strength to make my love fruitful in service.

Give me the strength never to disown the poor or bend my knees before insolent might.
Give me the strength to raise my mind high above daily trifles.
And Give me the strength to surrender my strength to thy will with love.

What a beautiful prayer? This prayer has been enlightening the minds of millions of people around the globe ever since it has been composed. Similarly, every prayer generates immense healing energy in mind, body and soul. Prayer is the most powerful technique to bring about mental, physical and spiritual healing. Prayer is the process of getting into an intimate feeling of connection with the Creator. Prayer can be a way of affirming our rightful desires. Prayer can be a source of drawing strength from an 'invisible source of power'. Our gratitude and thanksgivings may become our prayers.

Healing energy of prayer rejuvenates a person. It fills a person with hope, joy and love. Experiencing the healing energy of prayer at least once a day has its own advantages. Praying for strength indeed increases mental strength. It is always better to start a day with a short thanksgiving prayer. Prayer brings positive changes in all situations. It is said that *a family that prays together stays together.*

Prayer is the art of asking and receiving. As the Holy Bible says,

"Ask, and it will be given to you; seek, and you will find; knock, and it will be opened to you. For everyone who asks receives, and he who seeks finds, and to him who knocks it will be opened . . ." (Matthew 7:7-8)

The art of asking works in compliance with the universal law of attraction. A prayerful person is a highly energized person who is like strong magnet. Such persons can attract all that they pray for towards their life.

Prayers are positive affirmations of our rightful desires, our dreams, or our life's goals. In prayer we ask for the fulfillment of our rightful desires. For our prayers to be answered, we need ask specifically, and with belief until we get what we want. For the fulfillment of our desires we need to learn to visualize the fulfillment of our desire mentally, and then consciously feel the real manifestation of that desire in our life.

How to Achieve Fulfillment of Desires through Prayers and Positive Affirmations?

1. Take a stock of all your desires
2. Distinguish between right (positive) and wrong (negative) desires based on your value system
3. Eliminate all negative desires
4. Focus on only positive desires. Positive desires are your true desires.
5. Prioritize the desires in order of importance and necessity
6. Focus on the most important true desire now
7. Analyze whether the true desire is in harmony with the growth of your body, mind and spirit
8. During analysis focus on any hindering negative forces that block the realization of this desire
9. Major negative forces that hinders the realization of a true desire are—disbelief, doubts and fears, revenge and resentment, attachment and possessiveness, justification and rationalization, withholding and inability to let go, rejection and disappointment, defiance and resistance, submission, and sacrifice.
10. Try to eliminate all mental blocks by removing all negative forces by using the principles of love and forgiveness.
11. Achieve a mental state of calmness and perfect peace as a peaceful mind generates power for the realization of a desire.

Inner Peace through Silence and Solitude

The Hindu Scriptures mention about *ek tatva nirantar abhyas* (one pointed focus in silence on silence) and extols the virtue of silence as an important path to perfect living. Silence and solitude awakens the creative power within us. Absence of speech and noise creates a peaceful environment and a feeling of isolation. In such an environment it is easy to be left alone with one's own thoughts. In that aloneness one can find solitude, and solitude helps a person to attain an inner silence. In inner silence, a person begins *'self-discovery'*. In stillness of mind a person is able to seek God.

As the Book of Psalms says,

"Be still and know that I am God." (Psalm 46:10)

Inner Peace through Chanting *Mantras*

Chanting is the repetitive recitation of a holy word or a set of holy words (*mantra or japa*). A *mantra* or *japa* is a '*pure vibration*'. Therefore not all words are used as *mantras or japas*. Every religion has a set of holy words, by reciting which the believer experiences a feeling of healing and purification. Chanting the words of pure vibration repetitively and with focus purifies and heals a human being.

As the Hindu Scripture Sri Bhagavad Gita says,

"Verily nothing is more purifying than the holy name of God."

In Hinduism, the most celebrated mantra is the word, '*Ohm*'. Chanting may be done internally within our mind in silence or by producing the sound audibly while counting the number of intonations with the help of a *mala* (bead chain).

Inner Peace through Spending Time with Nature

Spending time with nature is a kind of worship. Being God's children, we are blessed with the most wonderful gift from God—Nature with all its creation. Nature glorifies God's love and peace in each of its elements. That is why, countryside sceneries, wilderness, woods and forests, flora and fauna, flowers, evening clouds, hills and mountains, lakes and rivers, all of these, instil a sense of peace within us. It is our responsibility to guard the treasures of the nature without disturbing its balance.

Inner Peace through Religion

The essence of a human being is the Spirit. So it is a human being's primary duty to keep the Spirit healthy. There is indeed a need for spiritual health. Religion and religious rituals help a person to keep the Spirit alive and healthy.

Every one of us is blessed with a religion; a religion into which we were born. We all are blessed with our religion's Holy Scriptures. All religions in the world are capable of directing their devotees on the *right path*. No one religion is superior to other. All religions are leading its devotees towards the same destination—*perfection*. The fundamental principles behind every religion are the same. These are, love, helping the poor (compassion), and altruism. So there is a need for all of us to respect all religions in the world.

As Sri Ramakrishna Paramahansa, renowned Hindu Saint says,

> *"All religions are true. The important thing is to reach the roof. You can reach it by stone stairs or by bamboo steps or by a rope. You can also climb up by a bamboo pole."*

It is always easy to practice the religion in which we are born because we grow up absorbing the teachings of that religion. We can easily relate our moral values with that of our religion in times of moral crisis. It is always advisable for us to believe in the religion in which we are born. We do not have to wander in search of right religion and right teachings if we devote to our religion wholeheartedly and understand the Scriptures of our religion. We only need to practice our religion with all devotion in order to find the truth and the right path. Practicing our religion and reading and contemplating on the Holy Scriptures help us gain worldly as well as spiritual wisdom.

As His Holiness the Dalai Lama says,

> *"You can appreciate all religions and at the same time maintain your own practice in whatever you have chosen to follow."*

Inner Peace through Religious Rituals

We need to actively participate in our religion's rituals. Religious rituals are meant for the worshipping of the Supreme Spirit (God). These religious rituals create such a sacred environment that the worshippers instantly feel a 'God connect' in that environment. These rituals are actually meant for mental and spiritual transformation of a devotee.

Religious rituals also help our 'individual spirit' to be in tune with the Supreme Spirit, thus activates the latent *'supreme energy'*, the source of all virtues and creativity, within us. Thus these rituals remind us the importance of practicing our core values in our day to day life. Religious rituals can have incredibly positive effect on a human being's mind, body and soul.

In the chapter of divine law of rhythms, we have read that the Hindu and the Buddhist philosophies believe in the concept of 'reincarnation' and 'cyclic existence'. According to Buddhist philosophy, liberation from cyclic existence is only possible through '*Three Jewels*'—the Master, the Teachings (the Scriptures) and the Spiritual Community. Belief in the Master and in his teachings is the only way to liberation. Every religion has a Master, *god manifestation in a human being* and its own Scriptures and teachings. Every religion has its followers (spiritual community). When we believe in the Master, we believe in His teachings. When we believe in His teachings, we follow Him and try our level best to put His teachings into practice. In the process of practicing the teachings of the Master, we purify ourselves and become closer to the Spirit.

Inner Peace through Harmony and Cooperation

A peaceful person is marked by lack of violence in speech and action. A peaceful person is blameless and upright in heart. A bright future awaits a man of peace. As the Book of Psalms says,

> "*Mark the blameless and behold the upright, for there is a future for the man of peace.*" (Psalm 37:37).

Peace is living in harmony with every element of the universe. Peace is cooperation and a peaceful person cooperates with other people for a good cause. A peaceful living is the beginning point of formation of a good society.

As Saint Paul says,

> "*If it is possible, as much as lieth in you, live peaceably with all men.*" (Romans 12:18)

A peaceful life begins the moment we determine to banish *hurry* and *worry* from our life; the moment we decide that we are not going to be worried about others' opinions and perceptions about us. Everybody has a right to free thinking and free speech. And they think and form opinions based on their perceptions. We cannot change their perceptions. People have a tendency to believe what they perceive. So let us live freely without being bothered about others' opinion about us. Let us live in peace with peaceful ways. As the Book of Proverbs says,

"When a man's ways please the Lord, he makes even his enemies to be at peace with him." (Proverbs 16:7).

Peaceful living is the best remedy for a stressful life. Inner peace eliminates all our stress, worries and anxieties of life. Inner peace allows a person to live in the moment.

As the Holy Bible says,

"Take therefore no thoughts for tomorrow, for the morrow shall take thought for itself." (Matthew 6:34).

This is the secret behind worry management.

10 Laws for Worry Management

1. Believe that you can change your worry (stress) habit
2. Decide that you will never be a 'Ms./Mr. Hurry Worry'
3. Never practice worry or stress. Instead practice self-belief
4. Believe you can, and you will
5. Make an action plan towards a 'stress-free' life
6. Utter silently many times a day that 'I hate my worry habit and I can change this habit'
7. Speak positive about everything
8. Never participate in negative speech that induces worries and stress
9. Be friendly with positive people
10. Practice prayer, meditation and positive affirmations

Inner Peace through Constant Renewal, Rest and Relaxation

Negative emotions, boredom with monotonous repetitive daily routine, laziness, negative people and negative circumstances drain a lot of energy from us. Sleep is the best remedy to recharge our 'positive' battery. Meditation, prayer and positive affirmations strengthen our minds. Play and exercise strengthen our body. Getting away to a holiday spot for a few days is also a wonderful form of relaxation.

Inner Peace through Good Company

Every human being has a desire to belong to a group of own kind. In order to have a sense of belonging to a group, people live in a society where they feel a sense of belonging and a cultural fit.
As the Book of Sirach says,

> *"Every creature prefers its own kind, and people are no different. Just as the animals of the same species flock together, so people keep company with people like themselves."*

This is the principle behind formation of clubs, associations and societies.

The level of refinement and civility differs with people. It is always a pleasure to interact with people who are as open-minded as we are; who share same interests that we have. It is a good experience to be in the society of similar-minded people. If one cannot find a good company, it is better off to be alone. The Holy Scriptures say that it is better to be alone than in a bad company.
As the Book of Sirach says,

> *"No one pities a person who associates with sinners"* (Sirach 12:13-14).

A bad company always brings negativity to a person through the power of absorption. The Holy Scriptures advise us to form friendships with only good people. As god's children, we all need to strive to be good human beings. A good human being is a carrier of manifested supreme energy. So it always gives us a great pleasure to be in the company of good people.
As Saint Paul says,

> *"Be not deceived: evil communications corrupt good manners."*
> (1 Corinthians 15:33).

It is a natural human tendency to focus on the negative more and to absorb it. Sometimes, we end up absorbing too much of negativity from the people around us. If we do not have a vent to release it, we too end up as negative persons with mental blocks, blocked love, peace and joy. A Spanish proverb goes like this, *"live with wolves and you will learn to howl."* Therefore we need to learn to eliminate negative people and toxic relationships from our life.

Inner Peace through Detachment and Renunciation

Detachment refers to the state of non-attachment to the fruits of one's own labour. Detachment is a state of renunciation where a person renounces his or her desires for things, people, wealth, or fame. That is, renunciation is a state of freedom from all cravings and desires. It is a state of inner freedom where a person is able to create more.

As Sri Ramakrishna Paramahansa, renowned Hindu Saint says,

> *"To work without attachment is to work without the expectation of reward or fear of any punishment in this world or the next. Work so done is a means to the end, and God is the end."*

Renunciation is an act of formal rejection of something as 'undesirable'. Since desire and associated attachment become bondages for a person, this attitude helps to be free in spirit.

As the Holy Bhagavad Gita says,

> *"By this attitude of complete renunciation you shall be freed from bondage, good and bad, of karma. You shall be liberated and come to me."*
> (Bhagawad Gita 9:28)

During this life journey, it is necessary that we should experience all that we wish to experience in this world. Otherwise our unfulfilled desires may become a hindrance to reach the path that we seek for. In the Scriptures, we may read about renunciations and sacrifices many times. But for an average human being, practicing the virtue of renunciation may be very difficult. For him/her, the path of renunciation may be a life that is deprived of good things of life.

As Indian poet Rabindranath Tagore says in *Gitanjali,*

"The traveller has to knock at every alien door to come to his own, and one has to wander through all the outer worlds to reach the innermost shrine at the end."

Inner Peace is the Secret behind Perception, Intuition, and Insight

Inner peace leads to intuition and insight into the future. Intuition is our sixth sense. Intuition is nothing but an inner knowing, without having any external evidence or proof to justify that knowledge. Intuition is inner perception.

An intuitive mind is a divine gift. It allows us to tap the life force at the brow chakra. As great scientist Albert Einstein says,

"The intuitive mind is a sacred gift and the rational mind is a faithful servant. We have created a society that honors the servant and has forgotten the gift."

CHAPTER 16

Personal Power System 7

"Nothing in this world purifies like spiritual wisdom. It is the perfection achieved in time through the path of yoga, the path that leads to the Self within".
(The Holy Bhagavad Gita 4:37-38)

*P*ersonal Power System 7 is the Power of Knowledge, Wisdom and Happiness.

Definition of Wisdom

Fear of God is the beginning of wisdom. Reading the Holy Scriptures and meditating on them is the surest way to grow in wisdom.
As Saint Paul says,

"The Sacred Scriptures are able to make you wise for salvation through faith in Jesus Christ. All Scriptures are God breathed and are useful for teaching, rebuking, correcting, and training in righteousness."
(2 Timothy 3:15-16).

Holy verses from the Holy Scriptures are the healthiest food for the Spirit. The Scriptures contain ageless wisdom of the Masters who have already walked on the earth. The Scriptures contain the *word* spoken by these Masters. Reading Scriptures is the only way to listen to the *word* of the Masters and learn wisdom from it.
As the Book of Psalms says,

"Your word is a lamp to my feet and a light to my path."
(Psalms 119:105).

What is Wisdom?

1. Wisdom is having right knowledge—knowledge about right and wrong (good and evil), knowledge of human nature and knowledge of the created universe
2. Wisdom is the ability to choose right experiences
3. Wisdom is choosing right over wrong
4. Wisdom is having discretion and prudence
5. Wisdom is having common sense and sound judgment
6. Wisdom is avoiding ignorance
7. Wisdom is having personal excellence

Wisdom is Discretion and Prudence

Prudence is the ability of being discreet and innocent while making decisions. *"Therefore be wise as serpents and harmless as doves."* (Matthew 10:16).

Prudence or discretion is the quality of being discreet, having common sense and sound judgment and being practically wise. It is the ability to choose between the right and the wrong.

Prudence tests everything but chooses only the right and the good. *"But test everything; hold fast what is good."* (1 Thessalonians 5:21).

Prudence respects authority. Prudence obeys all laws. Prudence teaches us that it is not wise to play power games with powerful people. *"Do not challenge a person who has influence; you may fall into his power."* (Sirach 8:1).

Power of Happiness

A merry heart produces happiness. Happy people are like fragrances. They spread the fragrance of their happiness all around them. We tend to believe that happy people are friendly, warm, selfless, and attractive. As the Book of Proverbs says,

"He that is of a merry heart hath a continual feast."

Happy people lighten our hearts with their smiles. As Thich Nhat Hanh, renowned Buddhist monk says,

"Sometimes your joy is the source of your smile; but sometimes your smile can be the source of your joy".

The source of a true smile is an awakened mind. In our daily life we can smile if we can be peaceful and happy, and not only we, but everyone will profit from it. According to group of psychologists, smiling produces the neurotransmitter serotonin, a vital component that regulates our mood, sleep and appetite. Laughter also produces endorphins, body's natural pain killers.

A smile is a smile, a true indicator of happiness. Smile is contagious. Smile is a universal language of love. Smiling helps us form healthy social relationships by creating positive first impressions. Smiling and friendly people convey the message that they are open, friendly, approachable and trustworthy. A person who is genuinely happy only gives a genuine smile. A genuine smile is reflected in the eyes of the person.

We all need to smile and laugh often. The law of smile and laughter is the law of happiness and joy. A smiling face conveys the message of pleasure and happiness. People with humor sense bring with them a lot of positive spirit. It is said that laughter is the medicine of soul and humor is the highest form of intelligence.

The happiest person is the one who constantly brings forth and practices what is best in her/him. Happiness and virtue complement each other. Not only are the best the happiest, but the happiest are usually the best at the art of perfect living. Happiness comes from a quiet mind. Meditating on peace, poise, security, and divine guidance brings happiness and joy.

A human lifetime is sufficient to experience true happiness. If we can achieve true happiness in this human life itself, then why can't we find it? We can begin this pursuit of happiness with our own family. Let us begin to love our spouse *unconditionally*, without any conditions or strings attached and feel the difference. Yes, we experience true happiness in our unconditional love. This true happiness enables us spread love throughout our family.

When our family is an abode of happiness, then every member of our family carries this happiness wherever they go. Now let us sit and silently watch this happiness spreading around. Remember, true happiness is birthright of every human being. True happiness begins when we realize that our happiness is not dependent on outer circumstances rather dependent on our inner goodness and greatness.

5 Laws of Joy and Happiness

1. Ability to tackle life's negative circumstances
2. Ability to handle frustration and rejection
3. Ability to handle relationships demands and financial pressure
4. Ability to tackle with life's disappointments and consequent complacent attitude
5. Ability to define life purpose and work towards it persistently

Need for Improvement and Constant Learning

One life time is not sufficient for us to learn everything and to know all that we want to know. There is always room for improvement. As Rabindranath Tagore says in Gitanjali,

"Ages pass, and still thou pourest, and still there is room to fill."

Normal human tendency is to acquire good enough education and sufficient life skills to live a comfortable life and then to settle down somewhere with a routine life. Such mediocre mentality does not believe in upgrading skills and acquiring more knowledge. They are not affected by the change of the world around them which is changing rapidly with rapid scientific and technological advancements. However, people who are intelligent and progress-oriented will always be eager to progress with the world around.

As the Book of Proverbs says,

"Intelligent people are always eager and ready to learn."
(Proverbs 18:15)

Education is life. Education brings empowerment. Empowerment brings freedom and independence. Therefore education is growth itself.

In case of children, education empowers them. Education imparts them with the skills and knowledge required to take the big responsibilities of an adult life. Most importantly, education makes the youth employable and empowers them to be a positive change in the society.

Education should be a lifelong process. This is the era of rapid technological progress. New inventions and discoveries are being made and new technologies are being used. Technologies are getting upgraded and old technologies are becoming outdated. So it is important that we update our professional knowledge and skills on a regular basis. We need to focus on constant learning but learn only that is necessary for our life's progress. Never try to learn everything or to know everything. There are a lot of contradictory information and viewpoints floating around us. We should never clutter our minds with wrong information and information overload. It is impossible to know everything about everything.

Life's experiences are different for different people. Therefore learning is also different. Everybody is God's favorite child and all of us need to learn our life lessons. Some have come a long way while others are still beginning with the basic lessons. But ultimately every one of us should become equal according to the plan of the Universe.

Learning from Mistakes

Great scientist Albert Einstein once remarked, *"Anyone who has never made a mistake has never tried anything new."* People are generally risk-averse. They are afraid of committing mistakes and trying something new by coming out of their comfort zone. The path to perfection is only for those who have the courage to take risks, make mistakes, admit the mistakes and rectify the mistakes at the earliest. According to India's national father M K Gandhi, *"Freedom is not worth having if it does not include the freedom to make mistakes."*

To err is human. Mistakes are a part of life and we should never regret about our past mistakes. Mistakes should be rectified but it should never become a part of our mental makeup. Regret and guilt feeling creates unnecessary mental tensions. If our mind is tensed our creativity is blocked.

Remember, there is always a second chance to get it right. It is better not to make mistakes. However, if at all, we make them unknowingly, correct our mistakes immediately. A person who commits same mistake more than twice is the biggest fool alive. Be ready to correct ourselves before correcting others.

As Atharva Veda, the Sacred Hindu Scriptures says,

"Scholars, learning from their mistakes of the past, plan their present and future accordingly and enjoy success, peace and prosperity."

The Pursuit of Happiness: The Art of Joyful Living

If we are images of God then our life is definitely a big event. Yes, *life is beautiful* and our life is the biggest gift from God. All *His* creation is here for us to enjoy and all *His* creation is good.

As Indian poet Rabindranath Tagore says in 'Gitanjali',

"Deliverance is not for me in renunciation. I feel the embrace of freedom in a thousand bonds of delight."

There is an *infinite intelligence* at work behind every creation. Human beings with their *limited intelligence* cannot measure the width and depth of this infinite intelligence. We need to stand in awe and wonder of the Creator of this creation. We need to celebrate our life with a joyful living. We need to rejoice in being fully alive. We need to rejoice in being fully free.

When we are free and fully alive, we become aware of all that is around us. We stand in awe of God's marvelous creations. There is a meaning behind every creation and we wonder at the thoughts that had gone behind every creation. We rejoice in the mysteries of life. We rejoice in the small pleasures of life—the sun rise and the sun set; the rivers and the woods; the butterflies and the birds; the rains and the snow fall; the breeze and the drizzle; and the flowers and the colors—everything excites us.

We need to learn from our life's experiences. Each life experience lets us grow and helps us to learn the truth behind it. When we know the truth we become liberated. This liberation is necessary for people like us to experience true happiness. Therefore we need to be open to all sorts of life experiences, both good and bad. It is said that *Variety is the Spice of Life*.

Progress towards perfection is possible only through such life-enriching experiences. Repetition or same mode of action does not bring in new experiences and related learning. Repetition creates monotony and such a life is stagnant. There is no further growth for such a life. So it is necessary for us to create a variety of life-enriching experiences so that we can live a rich life. We all have pure desires and we need to fulfill it by all rightful means.

Fulfillment of Pure Desires and Beautiful Life Experiences

Experiences are the truths of our life. We have experienced them and those experiences were truths. These truths strengthened us and gave us wisdom and courage to move forward.

Unfulfilled human desires sometimes are like big, heavy rocks on our path towards perfection. So it becomes imperative that we need to remove these obstacles from the path at any cost. That is, either fulfill these desires if these are legal and rightful or transmute this desire into a more acceptable and positive form. Fulfillment of a rightful desire creates a beautiful experience. When we experience a thing we know what it is. If it is not good for our growth we know how to overcome such experiences. And we learn from that experience and move forward. It is said that *experiences are our biggest teachers.*

Life's experiences are the essence of being human. These experiences are the mile stones that we enjoy most in the journey of life. Such experiences leave a trail of beautiful memories and *memories are forever.*

Actually people like us who are on the path of progression enjoy the journey towards perfection much more when we have such beautiful experiences and memories waiting for us along the path. Each experience indicates a turning point in our life and we take a better route to progress by learning valuable lessons from these life experiences.

Desires and temptations are not bad in themselves. But strength lies in not being tempted and at the same time, keeping a desireless mind.

As Saint Paul says,

"No temptation has overtaken you that is not common to man. God is faithful, and he will not let you be tempted beyond your ability, but with the temptation he will also provide the way of escape, that you may be able to endure it." (1 Corinthians 10:13)

Wrong desires are impure and bring us suffering. But right desires are pure in nature and propel us on the path of action. When we act on our desires, they become our purpose of life. Our desires become our motivations and inspirations to live a fruitful life, a life that becomes fruitful in service, and a life filled with creative action. Action brings the results that we desired for. Remember, *no action no results.*